Knits for Dogs & Cats

Knits for Dogs & Cats

By Tina Barrett

GUILD OF
MASTER CRAFTSMAN
PUBLICATIONS

First published 2006 by
Guild of Master Craftsman Publications Ltd
Castle Place, 166 High Street, Lewes, East Sussex
BN7 1XU

Photographs by Anthony Bailey

ISBN-13 978-1-86108-424-8
ISBN-10 1-86108-424-2

The publisher and author can accept no legal responsibility for any consequences arising from the application of information, advice or instructions given in this publication.

A catalogue record of this book is available from the British Library.

Production Manager: Hilary MacCallum
Managing Editor: Gerrie Purcell
Senior Project Editor: Dominique Page
Managing Art Editor: Gilda Pacitti
Animal Illustrations: Kath Walker
Knitting/Crochet Illustrations: Simon Rodway
Designer: Rebecca Mothersole

Set in Universe and Croissant
Colour origination by Altaimage
Printed and bound in Singapore by Kyodo

Dedicated to: My family and other animals. It's sometimes mayhem but I wouldn't have it any other way. Love you all!

The Basics

Contents

This book was inspired by two things: a lifelong obsession with all things knitting and a tall, skinny greyhound with bad breath and maddening habit of hijacking the sofa.

Introduction

We are a large family, the Barretts — one husband, three children, three dogs and a ferret. Unfortunately, my husband, supposed head of the household, is not great at being head of his pack. Consequently, our dogs are convinced they are human and I sit firmly at the bottom of their hierarchy, only slightly ahead of the ferret but some way below the children who play, fight and share biscuits with them on a regular basis.

Goldie, the aforementioned greyhound, passed her prime several summers ago and, despite her sofa-hogging tendencies, became a very much-loved part of our family. Last winter, her advanced years made her understandably reluctant to leave the warm, cosy house for her regular walks on the moor. 'Knit her a jumper', suggested my husband, quickly adding, 'just make sure it's not embarrassing'.

And so this book was born. I searched high and low for 'non-embarrassing' dog sweater patterns. There were many colourful and fun versions available but none suitable for the more macho dog-walker like my husband. It struck me that pet owners really do prefer it when their animals reflect their own tastes and even clothing choices. Perhaps — like the old saying goes — dog owners really do want their dogs to look like them.

So, with this in mind, I set about designing that sweater for Goldie and my sports-mad husband. Eventually, I came up with a red, striped tracksuit top. It turned out to be a winner. It fitted, looked good, she wore it and my husband walked her without a murmur.

Sadly, Goldie has since passed on to that great sofa in the sky, and there is a huge gap in our front room that will take some time to adjust to. But the jumper incident got me thinking, and so I carried on knitting until I produced a whole range of sweaters and accessories to suit pet owners and their lifestyles.

The results lie in these pages: twenty-five sweaters and accessories for urban and country living. I really hope you like them. Indeed, I hope you find something 'non-embarrassing' to knit for your loved ones, be they two-legged or four.

2

Second Class To make the projects with this difficulty rating you will only need basic knitting skills.

They are suitable for the complete beginner.

First Class Projects with this difficulty rating are not so easy.

1

But, even if you are new to knitting, you can give them a go – you'll find all the information you need in 'Knitting Essentials' at the back of the book.

Knitwear

For Dogs

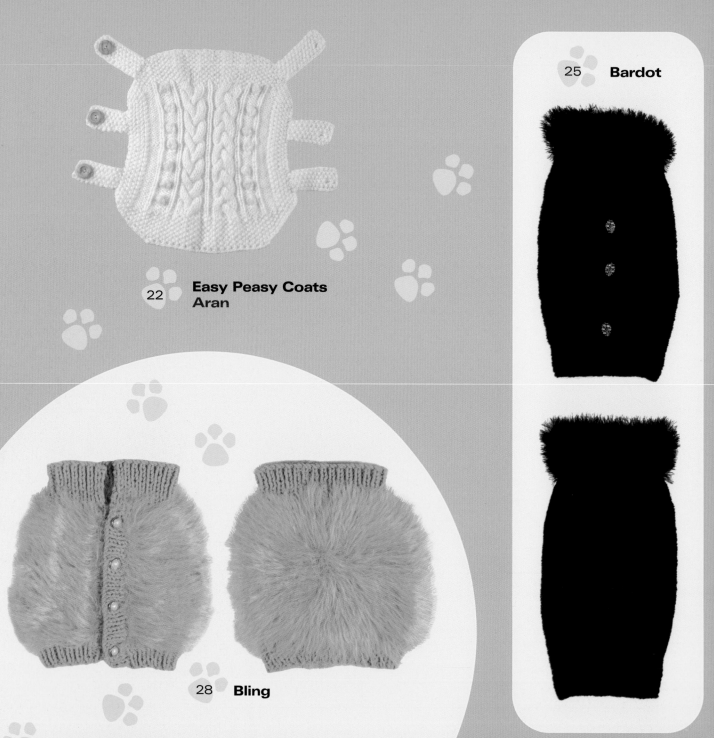

22 **Easy Peasy Coats Aran**

25 **Bardot**

28 **Bling**

31 **Flower**

Fetch!

Follow Mutley's paw prints to see each project

31 **Flower**

20 **Easy Peasy Coats**
Denim Stripe

34 **Tiffany**

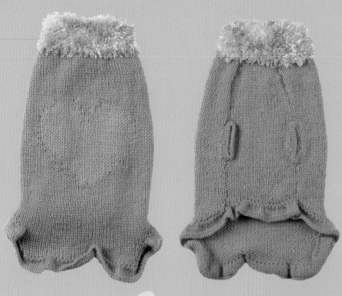

43 **Heart**

62 **Mod Parka**

40 **Ballerina**

Park Life

48

Beaded 36

59 **Combat**

56 **Punk Vibe**

71 **Fair Isle**

52 **Trackie**

67 **Diamond Guy**

Unisex Doggywear

Easy Peasy
Coats

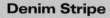

This coat really is easy peasy to make. It consists of one rectangular panel, which you can adjust to any length, with button-through straps for a custom fit.

Denim Stripe

Materials and Equipment
❧ Sirdar Luxury Soft Cotton Dk in:
French Navy,
2[2:3:3] 1³⁄₄oz (50g) balls
Venetian Blue,
1[1:2:2] 1³⁄₄oz (50g) balls
❧ 4mm (US 6) needles
❧ 3 jeans buttons

Tension
22 sts x 28 rows to 4in (10cm)

Sizing
S[M:L:XL]
Chest: 14[18:22:26]in
(36[46:56:66]cm)
Length: 12[16:21:23]in
(30.5[41:53.5:58.5]cm)

Main Panel
Using French Navy and
4mm (US 6) needles CO
44[54:66:76] sts.
Row 1: *K1, P1 * rep from * to *
to end.
Row 2: * P1, K1* rep from * to *
to end.
These two rows set the moss
stitch border pattern. Keeping moss
stitch patt, inc into first and last
stitch of next and every following
row until 66[76:88:98] sts (13
rows in total).

Row 14: Moss st whole row
without increasing.
Still using French Navy begin Stripe
Patt as follows:
Row 15: Moss st 6 sts, K to last 6
sts, moss st to end.
Row 16: Moss st 6 sts, p to last 6
sts, moss st to end.
Rep these last 2 rows twice more
(6 rows in total).
Next Row: Moss st 6 sts, change
to Venetian Blue and K to last 6
sts, change to French Navy and
moss st to end.
Next Row: In French Navy, moss st
6 sts, change to Venetian Blue and

p to last 6 sts, change to French
Navy and moss st to end.
Rep these last two rows twice
more (6 rows in total).
These 12 rows form the stripe
sequence. Keep repeating them
until work measures 10[14:19:21]in
(25.5[35.5:48.5:53.5]cm) ending
on a WS row.
*If you need to shorten or lengthen the coat,
do it now before proceeding to the next
part of the pattern.*
Change or keep to French Navy.
Moss st straight across the next
two rows. Decrease for lower
border as follows:
Keeping to moss st patt, K2tog at
the beg and end of next and every
following row until 44[54:66:76]
sts. Cast off loosely in moss st.

Straps – Make 3
Using French Navy and 4mm (US
6) needles CO 8 sts.
** **Row 1**: *K1, P1 * rep from * to *
to end.
Row 2: * P1, K1 * rep from * to *
to end**.
Rep these two rows until work
measures 4[4:5:5]in
(10[10:13:13]cm).
Cast off in moss st.

Buttonhole Straps – Make 3

Using French Navy and 4mm needles CO 8 sts.
Works as for straps from ** to **.
Rep these two rows until work measures 3[3:4:4]in (8[8:10:10]cm) ending on a WS row.
Next Row: K1, P1, K1, YO, K2tog, P1, K1, P1.
Next Row: *P1, K1 * rep from * to * to end.
Work even in moss st until strap measures 4[4:5:5]in (10[10:13:13]cm).
Cast off in moss st.

Making Up

Darn in any loose ends and pin straps onto main panel according to the diagram (right). Try onto your dog. Adjust strap placement to fit and mark button position on straps with a pin. Remove and sew straps firmly in place. Sew buttons on and away you go!

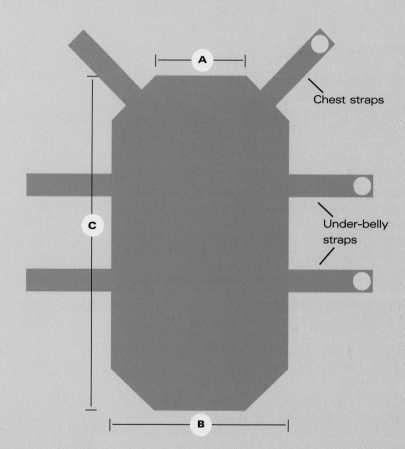

Chest straps

Under-belly straps

A 8[10:12:14]in (20.5[25.5:30.5:35.5]cm)

B 12[14:16:18]in (30.5[35.5:41:46]cm)

C 12[16:21:23]in (30.5[41:53.5:58.5]cm)

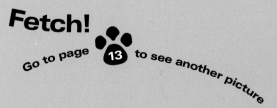

Fetch!

Go to page 13 to see another picture

It may seem contradictory to have an easy peasy coat with a First Class skill rating but I will explain.

The coat is constructed in the same, simple way as the Denim Stripe but is worked in cable instead – a more difficult technique.

Aran

Materials and Equipment
❖ Robin Aran in Aran 1871
   1 x 14oz (400g) ball
❖ 5mm (US 8) needles
❖ 3 wooden buttons
❖ Cable needle

Tension
19 sts x 24 rows to 4in (10cm)

Sizing
As for Denim Stripe

Special Instructions
MB: Make bobble as follows: (K1, p1) twice into next st, turn, P4, turn, K4, turn, K2tog twice, turn, K2tog. 6 sts cbfr: sl 3 sts to cn and hold to front of work, K3, K3 from cn 6 sts cbbk: sl 3 sts to cn and hold to back of work, K3, K3 from cn.

Main Panel
Using Robin Aran and 5mm (US 8) needles CO 39[47:59:67] sts.
Row 1: * K1, P1 * rep from * to * to end.
Row 2: * K1, P1* rep from * to * to end. Keeping to the moss st patt as set, inc 1 st into first and last st of next and every following row until 61[69:81:89] sts (13 rows in total).

Row 14: Moss st without increasing.
Now find your dog's size on the cable chart, on page 23, and beg working the 8 row reps. Carry on until coat measures 10[14:19:21]in (25.5[35.5:48.5:53.5]cm) ending on a WS row.
If you need to shorten or lengthen the coat, do it now before proceeding to the next part of the pattern. Moss st straight across the next two rows.

Decrease for border edge as follows:
Keeping to moss st patt, K2tog at beg and end of next and every foll row until 39[47:59:67] sts.
Cast off in moss st.

Finishing
Tidy up any loose yarn ends. Using 5mm (US 8) needles and Robin Aran make straps as for Denim Stripe. Follow previous instructions to fit and finish (see page 21).

Fetch!
Go to page  **12** to see another picture

Actually, cable is easier than many beginners realize and it's well worth giving this pattern a go, as there are very few shapings to worry about so you can just get on with mastering the twists and bobbles. For a guide to following cable charts, see 'Knitting Essentials', page 123.

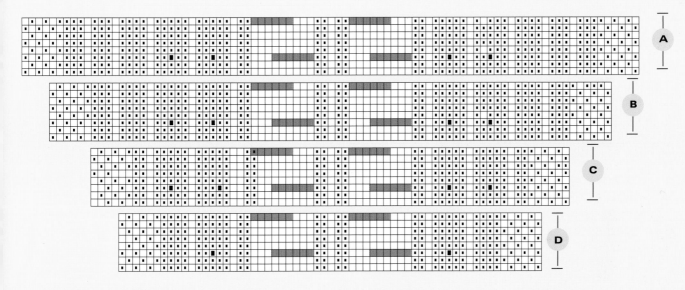

Key

○ P on RS, K on WS

⊡ K on Rs, P on WS

■ MB – make bobble

● 6 sts cbfr

● 6 sts cbbk

A Extra large: 8 rows x 89 sts

B Large: 8 rows x 81 sts

C Medium: 8 rows x 69 sts

D Small: 8 rows x 61 sts

One square = 1 st + 1 row

Fashionable Females

Bardot

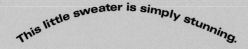

This little sweater is simply stunning.

Materials and Equipment

* Wendy Velvet Touch in Midnight-shade 2007, 1[1:2] x 1¾oz (50g) balls
* Patons Whisper DK in Jet-shade 00007, 1[1:1] x 1¾oz (50g) balls
* 4.5mm (US 7) and 4mm (US 6) needles
* Stitch holder
* 2[3:4] diamanté buttons

Tension

19 sts x 30 rows to 4in (10cm) using Velvet Touch and 4.5mm (US 7) needles
22 sts x 30 rows to 4in (10cm) using Patons Whisper and 4mm (US 6) needles

Sizing

XS[S:M]
Chest: 10[14:18]in (25.5[35.5:46]cm)
Actual: 11[15:19]in (28[38:48.5]cm)
Length: 9[12:16]in (23[30.5:41]cm)

Top Panel *(neck to bottom)*

Using 4.5mm (US 7) needles and Wendy Velvet Flake CO 38[48:58] sts.
Begin patt as follows:
Row 1: K16[22:27], P4,

K16[22:27].
Row 2: P16[22:27], K4, P16[22:27].
Rep these 2 rows until work measures 5[8:12]in (13[20.5:30.5]cm) ending on a WS row.
Adjust length here if required.
Dec as follows:
Keeping to patt, K2tog at each end of next and every alt. row until 18[28:48] sts.
Now cont in patt until work measures 9[12:16]in (23[30.5:41]cm) ending on a WS row.
Cast off.

Under Panel *(bottom to neck)*

Using 4.5mm (US 7) needles and Wendy Velvet Flake CO 14[20:24] sts.
Work even in st st until work measures 4[7:10]in (10[18:25.5]cm) ending on a WS row.
Adjust length here if required.
Dec for neck as follows:
K2tog at each end of next and every foll row until 8[8:8] sts.
Work even in st st until under panel measures 5[8:12]in (13[20.5:30.5]cm) ending on a WS row. Leave sts on a holder.

Collar

With RS facing, using 4mm (US 6) needles and Patons Whisper, PUK 36[46:58] sts along neck edge of Top Panel.
Now K across the sts on the stitch holder of the Under Panel. The two pieces should be sitting side by side on one needle. 44[54:66] sts in total.
Row 1: P.
Row 2: Inc as follows: K7[2:2], *M1, K2* rep from * to * until last 7[0:0] sts, K to end.
60[80:98] sts in total.
Row 3: P.
Row 4: K.
Rep rows 3 and 4 until collar

measures 3[3.5:4.5]in (8[9:11.5]cm) ending on a P row.
Cast off loosely in garter st.

Making Up

Sew in any loose ends and, with RS facing, pin and sew collar and side seams leaving 2[2.5:3]in (5[6.5:8]cm) opening on each side for leg openings 3[4:5]in (8[10:13]cm) down from beneath the collar seam.

Top Panel

Turn down collar to RS and then measure and sew diamanté buttons firmly onto the centre panel of front to finish.

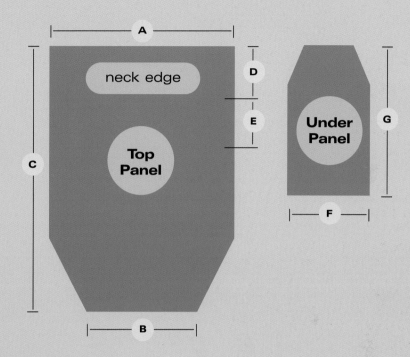

neck edge

Top Panel

Under Panel

Fetch!
Go to page 12 to see more pictures

Top Panel

A 7[11:14]in (18[28:35.5]cm)

B 4[6:10]in (10[15.5:25.5]cm)

C 9[12:16]in (23[30.5:41]cm)

D 3[4:5]in (8[10:13]cm)

E 2[2.5:3]in (5[6.5:8]cm)

Under Panel

F 3[4:5]in (8[10:13]cm)

G 5[8:12]in (13[20.5:30.5]cm)

Bling

Materials and Equipment

- Saprotex Gold Chunky in Blush, 1 x 3½oz (100g) ball
- Elle Sensual Shade 261, 2[3] x 1¾oz (50g) balls
- 5mm (US 8) needles
- 4.5mm (US 7) dpns
- Stitch holder
- 4 buttons

Tension

Using Saprotex Gold Chunky and 5mm (US 8) needles, 15 sts x 21 rows to 4in (10cm)

Using Elle Sensual and 5mm (US 8) needles, 22 sts x 30 rows to 4in (10cm)

Sizing

S[M]

Chest: 14[18]in (35.5[46]cm)
Actual: 16[20]in (41[51]cm)
Length: 10[14]in (25.5[35.5]cm)

Pattern *(from bottom up)*

Using Saprotex Gold Chunky and 5mm (US 8) needles CO 60[75] sts.

Row 1: *K1, P1* rep from * to * to end.

Row 2: * K1, P1 * rep from * to * to end.

These two rows form the rib pattern. Rep until work measures 1[2]in (2.5[5]cm) ending on a row 2. Change to Elle Sensual.

Next Row:

Small Size Only: K3 * M1, K2 * rep from * to * until last 3 sts, K to end. (88 sts).

Medium Size Only: K4, * M1, K2 * rep from * to * until last 4 sts, K to end (110 sts).

All Sizes: P.

Now work in st st until coat measures 2[4]in (5[10]cm) from beg ending on a WS row.

Adjust length here if required.

Divide for legs as follows:

Next Row: K17[22] sts, using a separate ball of yarn K54[66] sts, and finally using another separate ball of yarn K17[22] sts.

Now continue to work these three pieces separately in st st until they measure 3in (8cm), ending on a

WS row. Break 2nd and 3rd balls of yarn. Using first ball of yarn knit straight across the three pieces and continue to work in st st until coat measures 10[14]in (25.5[35.5]cm) ending on a WS row.

Decrease for neck as follows:

Small Size Only: K6, * K2tog * rep from * to * until last 6 sts, K to end (50 sts).

Medium Size Only: K5, *K2tog * rep from* to * until last 5 sts, K to end (60 sts).

All Sizes: P.

Leave rem sts on stitch holder.

Right Front Border

**With RS facing and using Saprotex Gold and 5mm (US 8) needles, PUK 36(52) sts up the right front edge of coat.

Row 1: *K1, P1* rep from * to * to end.

Row 2: * K1, P1* rep from * to * to end. **

These two rows form the rib patt. Rep once more (4 rows in total). Cast off in rib.

Now mark button placements on this border.

Left Front Border

Rep as for right front border from ** to **.

Row 3: Taking note of the button positions on the right front band

Even the humblest mongrel will look a million dollars wearing this little number.

All you need now is someone who can afford you both...

work the rib patt as set but making four buttonholes at regular intervals as follows: YO, K2tog.
Row 4: As row 2.
Cast off in rib.

Collar

With RS facing and using Saprotex Gold and 5mm (US 8) needles, PUK 4 sts from top edge of right front band, K across the sts from stitch holder and PUK 4 sts from top edge of left front band. 58[68] sts.
Row 1: *K1, P1 * rep from * to * to end.
Row 2: * K1, P1 * rep from * to * to end.
These two rows form the rib patt. Rep until collar measures 2[3]in (5[8]cm).
Cast off loosely in rib.

Leg Openings

With RS facing and using Saprotex Gold and dpns, PUK 18 sts around first leg opening. Rib as for collar for 2 rows. Cast off loosely. Rep for second leg.

Finishing

Darn in loose ends and sew buttons on firmly. Tease out the fur and brush through with fingers for a fluffy, luxurious finish.

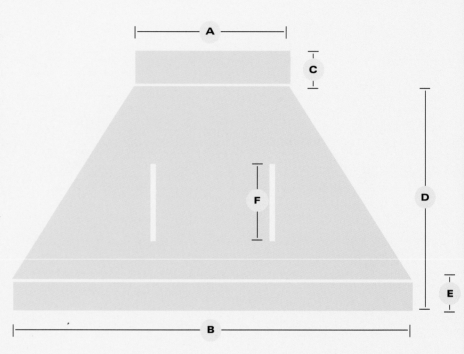

A 9[11]in (23[28]cm)

B 16[20]in (41[51]cm)

C 2[3]in (5[8]cm)

D 10[14]in (25.5[35.5]cm)

E 1[2]in (2.5[5]cm)

F 3in (8cm)

Fetch!

Go to page 12 to see more pictures

Flower

This pretty flower design is so quick and easy to make. Knitted in Aran and decorated with a few simple felt flowers, your friends will think you're a knitting genius.

Materials and Equipment

- Stylecraft Aran in Hydrangea, 1 x 14oz (400g) ball
- 5mm (US 8) needles
- Set of 5 dpns or 5mm (US 8) 23½in (60cm) circular needles (for larger size only)
- Stitch holder
- Pink/pale pink felt squares
- Selection of pearl beads

Tension

18 sts x 24 rows to 4in (10cm)

Sizing

XS[S:M]

Chest: 10[14:18]in (25.5[35.5:46]cm)
Actual: 11[15:19]in (28:38:48.5]cm)
Length: 9[12:16]in (23[30.5:41]cm)

Top Panel *(bottom upwards)*

Using Stylecraft Aran and 5mm (US 8) needles CO 26[44:54] sts. Work 2 rows in st st.
Row 3 (and every further 4th row): Inc into first and last st of row 28[46:54] sts.
Cont in st st, inc on every 4th row as set until 36[54:64] sts.
Now work until the coat measures 8[11:15]in (20.5[28:38]cm) ending on a WS row.

Adjust length here if required.
Decrease for neck as follows:
Next Row: K11[9:8] sts, *K2tog * rep from * to * until last 11[9:8] sts. K to end. 29[36:40] sts in total.
Next Row: P.
Leave rem sts on stitch holder.

Under Panel

Using Stylecraft Aran and 5mm (US 8) needles CO 14[18:22] sts. Work in st st until coat measures 5[8:12]in (13[20.5:30.5]cm) ending on a WS row.
Adjust length here if required.
Decrease for neck as follows:
Next Row: *K2tog * rep from * to * to end of row. 7[9:11] sts in total.
Next Row: P.
Leave rem sts on stitch holder.

Neck

With RS facing, using Aran and 5mm (US 8) needles, K across the stitch holder of the top panel and then the under panel. The two pieces should be sitting side by side on one needle. 36[45:51] sts in total.
Next Row: K.
Next Row: K into front and back of every st 72[90:102] sts in total.
Next Row: P.
Cont in st st until neck measures 1in (3cm) ending on a RS row.
Next Row: K.
Next Row: Cast off in garter st.

Interim Making Up

Fold the two pieces in half lengthways with RS facing.
Sew up the neck and side seam, leaving a 2.5in (6.5cm) leg opening, 3[4:5]in (8[10:13]cm) from the bottom edge of the collar.
Rep for second seam.

Lower Edging

With RS facing, using circular needles or dpns and Aran, PUK 14[18:22] st from bottom edge of under panel, 18 sts along right side edge, 26[44:54] sts across bottom of top panel, 18 st down left side edge. 76[98:112] sts in total.

Round 1: P.

Round 2: K into the front and back of every st. 152[196:224] sts in total.

Next and every foll round: K. Rep until frill measures 1in (2.5cm).

Next Row: P.

Next Row: Cast off purlwise.

Finishing

Neaten yarn ends. Then taking your templates cut out three small pale pink felt flowers, two small pink flowers and one large pink flower. Arrange four of the small flowers on the lower edge of the sweater — slightly towards the right-hand side. Pin and sew in place. Use beads to decorate the flower centres. Take the large pink flower and position at the left-hand side of the neck edge. Place the smaller flower in the centre. Pin and sew in place. Again, decorate with beads.

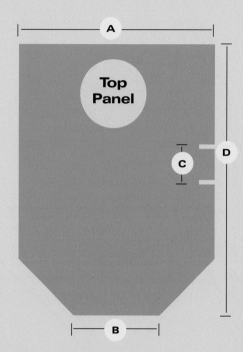

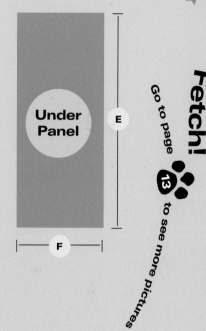

Fetch! Go to page 13 to see more pictures

Top Panel

A 8[12:14]in (20.5[30.5:35.5]cm)

B 6[10:12]in (15.5[25.5:30.5]cm)

C 2.5in (6.5cm)

D 9[12:16]in (23[30.5:41]cm)

Under Panel

E 5[8:12]in (13[20.5:30.5]cm)

F 3[4:5]in (8[10:13]cm)

Flower Template

Reproduce at 200% for the large flower and at 100% for the others.

Tiffany

This glamorous fur cape is perfect for those red-carpet occasions when you and your baby simply must dazzle the paparazzi!

Materials and Equipment

- ❖ Stylecraft Icicle in Pink, 1 x 1¾oz (50g) ball
- ❖ Jaeger Matchmaker Merino 4-ply in pink, small amount
- ❖ 4mm (US 6) needles

Tension

22 sts x 30 rows to 4in (10cm)

Sizing

XS/S

Pattern

Using Icicle and 4mm (US 6) needles CO 50 sts.

St st for 5 rows.

Row 6: Inc 1 st into first and last st of row (52 sts).

Continue working in st st but **at the same time** working the increase row as set on every 5th row until 66 sts.

Now work until work measures 6in (15cm) from beginning, ending on a WS row.

To work the bottom shaping, decrease one st at each end of the next and every alt. row until you have 50 sts remaining.

Cast off 10 sts at beginning of next 5 rows.

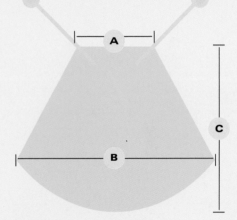

Designed for the smaller dog, it's simple to make but looks really special.

Finishing

Using the Jaegar 4-ply, make two twisted cords about 5in (13cm) in length. Now make two small pompoms in Icicle and sew firmly to the ends of the neckties. Sew the ties to the neck corners and head for that premiere!

- Ⓐ 9in (23cm) wide
- Ⓑ 13in (33cm)
- Ⓒ 8in (20.5cm)

Fetch! Go to page ⓭ to see another picture

Beaded

Materials and Equipment

- Rowan 4-ply Soft in 377 Wink or 370 Whisper, 2[2:3:5] x 1¾oz (50g) balls
- E size Impex Trimits Grosse Rocaille beads in Pearl and Pink, approx. 100[220:390:630]
- 3.25mm (US 3) needles
- 3.25mm (US 3) 23½in (60cm) circular needles
- 5 dpns
- Stitch holder
- Beading needle

Tension

28 sts x 36 rows to 4in (10cm)

Sizing

XS[S:M:L]

Chest: 10[14:18:22]in (25.5[35.5:46:56]cm)

Actual: 11[15:19:24]in (28[38:48.5:61]cm)

Finished Length: 9[12:16:21]in (23[30.5:41:53.5]cm)

Special Instructions (Beading Patt):

Rows 1–4: St st.

Row 5: K4 *yf, sl1p. mb, yb, K5* rep from * to * until last 2[6:3:1] sts, K to end.

Row 6: P.

Rows 7–10: St st.

Row 11: K2 *yf, sl1p, mb, yb, K5* rep from * to * until last 4[1:5:3]

sts, K to end.

Row 12: P.

These 12 rows form the bead pattern worked throughout the top panel.

Top Panel

First, using a beading needle, thread beads onto a ball of Rowan 4-ply Soft.

Using 3.25mm (US 3) needles CO 49[77:98:126] sts.

Work Bead Patt for 5[8:12:16]in (13[20.5:30.5:41]cm) and end on a P row.

Adjust length here if required.

Next, keeping to Bead Patt, K2tog at each end of next and every alt row until 35[49:70:98] sts.

Continue working straight in Bead Patt until work measures 8.5[11.5:15.5:20.5]in (21.5[29.5:39.5:52]cm) and end on a P row.

Leave sts on a stitch holder.

Bottom Panel

Using 3.25mm (US 3) needles and Rowan 4-ply Soft CO 22[28:36:42] sts.

Row 1: K6[5:7:8] *P2, K2 * rep from * to * 2[4:5:6] times, P2, K6[5:7:8].

Row 2: P6[5:7:8] *K2, P2 * rep from * to * 2[4:5:6] times, K2, P6[5:7:8].

Rep these 2 rows as set until work measures 4[7:10:14]in (10[18:25.5:35.5]cm) ending on a WS row.

Adjust length here if required.

Keeping to rib patt as set, K2tog at each end of next and every alt row until 10[18:22:26] sts.

Work in patt until work measures 5[8:12:16]in (13[20.5:30.5:41]cm) ending on a WS row.

Leave sts on needle.

Just thread the beads onto the yarn using a beading needle...

Collar

Using the other 3.25mm (US 3) needle, Rowan 4-ply Soft and with RS of top panel facing, PUK 46[48:58:78] sts along the neck edge.

Now, keeping to the rib patt as already set, rib across the sts of the bottom panel that are waiting on your other needle. The two pieces should now be sitting side by side on one needle, 53[66:80:104] sts in total.

Next Row (WS) : Starting with P2, work P2, K2 rib right the way across the whole row.

Cont in rib for 1[1.5:2:2.5]in (3[4:5:6.5]cm) and cast off loosely in rib.

Interim Making Up

Fold your work in half and with RS facing, sew up the two side seams leaving 2[2.5:3:3.5]in (5[6.5:8:9]cm) openings, 3[4:5:7]in (8[10:13:18]cm) down from the bottom of the collar.

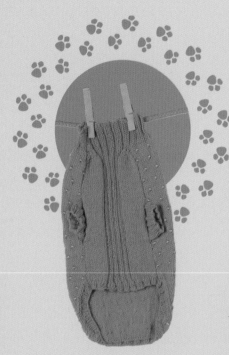

Legs

Using set of 4 dpns, Rowan 4-ply Soft and with RS facing, PUK 30[36:48:54] sts around the leg opening.

St st (i.e. every round garter st) for 0.5[0.5:1.5:2.5]in (1.5[1.5:4:6.5]cm) then change to K2, P2 rib for 4 rounds. Cast off loosely in rib. Rep for other leg.

Bottom Edge

Using set of 5 dpns for smaller sizes or circular needle for larger size and Rowan 4-ply Soft begin picking up sts from the right-hand seam edge of the bottom panel and proceed as follows:

PUK 21[27:36:42] sts across bottom panel, 24 sts across right side edge, 35[49:70:98] sts from stitch holder, 24 sts down left-side edge. 104[124:154:188] sts in total.

Work 4 rounds in K2, P2 rib.

Cast off loosely in rib and darn in any loose ends.

Fetch! Go to page 15 to see more pictures

.... or if you can't find a needle fine enough then try using a small length of fuse wire bent over at one end to make an eye.

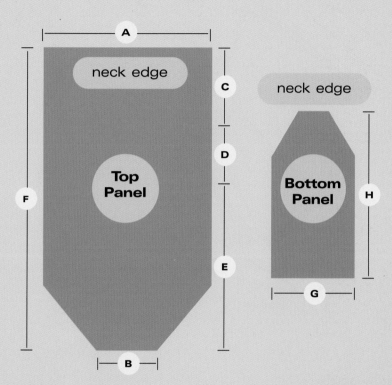

A

neck edge

C

D

Top Panel

E

F

B

neck edge

Bottom Panel

H

G

Top Panel

A 7[11:14:18]in
(18[28:35.5:46]cm)

B 5[7:10:14]in
(13[18:25.5:35.5]cm)

C 3[(4:5:7]in
(8[10:13:18]cm)

D 2[2.5:3:3.5]in
(5[6.5:8:9]cm)

E 4[5.5:8:10.5]in
(10[14.5:20.5:26.5]cm)

F 9[12:16:21]in
(23[30.5:41:53.5]cm)

Bottom Panel

G 3[4:5:6]in
(8[10:13:15.5]cm)

H 5[8:12:16]in
(13[20.5:30.5:41]cm)

Ballerina

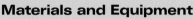

This sweet ballerina-style wrap is knitted in a pretty cloverleaf lace pattern and tied with a satin ribbon.

Materials and Equipment
- ❖ Patons 100% DK cotton in Shade 02711 Ocean, 2 x 3½oz (100g) balls
- ❖ 3.25mm (US 3) and 4mm (US 6) needles
- ❖ 5 x 3.25mm (US 3) dpns or 23½in (60cm) circular needle
- ❖ 3⅓ft (1m) of 1in (2.5cm) wide, pale blue satin ribbon

Tension
22 sts x 30 rows over 4in (10cm)

Sizing
S/M
Chest: 14–16in (35.5–41cm)
Length: 11in (28cm)

Cloverleaf Lace Pattern
Row 1 and every alt row (WS): P to end.
Row 2 (RS): K to end.
Row 4 : K2, yfwd, sl 1, K2tog, psso, yfwd, *K5, yfwd, sl 1, K2tog, psso, yfwd; rep from * to last 2 sts, K2.
Row 6 : K3, yfwd, sl 1, K1, psso, *K6, yfwd, sl 1, k1, psso; rep from * to last 2 sts, K2.
Row 8: K to end.
Row 10: K1 *K5, yfwd, sl 1, K2tog, psso, yfwd; rep from * to last 6 sts, K6.
Row 12: K7 *yfwd, sl 1, K1, psso,

K6; rep from * to end.
Rows 1–12 form the pattern.

Main Body *(bottom to neck)*
Using 3.25mm (US 3) needles and Ocean CO 127 sts.
Row 1: *K1, P1* rep from * to * to end.
Row 2: *P1, K1 * rep from * to * to end.
Rep these 2 rib rows once more (4 rows in total). Change to 4mm (US 6) needles.
Work row 1 of cloverleaf lace pattern.

Keeping to patt, work ribbon opening as follows:
Row 2: Patt 32, cast off 4 sts, patt to end.
Row 3: Patt 95, CO 4 sts, patt to end.
Row 4 and every alt row: K2tog, patt to last 2 sts, K2tog.
Now continue working in patt while **at the same time**, working the decreases at the outer edges as set on row 4 until 105 sts ending on a WS row.

Divide for Legs
Next Row: patt 25, attach a new of ball of yarn, patt 55, attach a new ball of yarn, patt 25.
Now, **keeping to patt and continuing decreases**, work these three sections separately until they measure 3in (8cm) ending on a WS row.
Next Row: Using one ball of yarn only, patt right across the row and cont working on the whole garment as before.
Keep working in patt, continuing the decreases until 61 sts remain. Now, still keeping to patt, work the decreases on every row until 53 sts ending on a RS row.
Decrease for neck as follows:
*P3, P2 tog, * rep from * to * to end. 43 sts in total.
Leave rem sts on a holder.

You may have to concentrate a little more with lace knitting, but once you've got the repeats going you'll be away and, as I'm sure you'll agree, the resulting wrap is so cute, it's well worth it.

Neckband

With RS facing and using either 3.25mm (US 3) dpns or circular needles and Ocean, PUK 50 st along right front band, K across the 43 sts of st holder at neck and 50 st down the left front band. 143 sts in total.

Row 1: *K1, P1* rep from * to * to end.

Row 2: * P1, K1 * rep from * to * to end.

Rep these 2 rib rows once more (4 rows in total).

Cast off loosely in rib.

Legs

With RS facing and using 3.25mm (US 3) dpns and Ocean, PUK 38 sts around leg opening.

Round 1: * K1, P1 * rep from * to * to end.

Rep this rib round 3 more times (4 rounds in total) then cast off loosely in rib.

Rep for other leg.

Finishing

Tidy up loose yarn ends and then press lightly. Cut the ribbon in half and sew firmly to the bottom inside edges of ribbing. Try the wrap on your dog and then tie and cut the ribbon to length.

Fetch! Go to page **15** to see more pictures

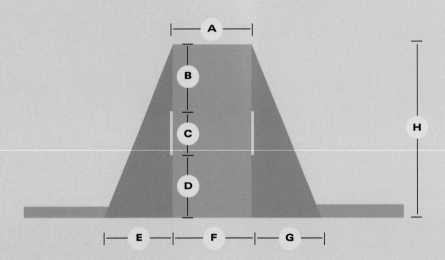

A 10in (25.5cm)	**E** 5in (13cm)
B 4in (10cm)	**F** 10in (25.5cm)
C 3in (8cm)	**G** 5in (13cm)
D 4in (10cm)	**H** 11in (28cm)

Heart

Materials and Equipment

- Elle Plume in Fairy Floss, shade 215, 1 x 1¾oz (50g) ball
- Patons Diploma Gold in:
  Iris, shade 06231,
  1[2:2] x 1¾oz (50g) ball
  Hollyhock, shade 06158,
  1 x 1¾oz (50g) ball
- 4mm (US 6) needles
- 4mm (US 6) 5dpns or 23½in (60cm) circular needle
- Stitch holder

Tension

18 sts x 26 rows to 4in (10cm) with Elle Plume and 4mm (US 6) needles
22 sts x 30 rows to 4in (10cm) with Patons Diploma Gold and 4mm (US 6) needles

Sizing

XS[S:M]

Chest: 10[14:18]in (25.5[36:46]cm)
Actual: 11[15:1]in (28[38:48.5]cm)
Length: 9[12:16]in (23[30.5:41]cm)

Top Panel (neck downwards)

Using Iris and 4mm (US 6) needles CO 38[60:76] sts.
Working in st st, work 8[20:40] rows ending on a WS row.
Start working from row 1 of the intarsia chart (page 46):
Row 1: K5[16:24], work 28 sts from chart, K5[16:24] sts.

Row 2: P5[16:24], work 28 sts from chart, P5[16:24].
When you have finished the heart pattern, cont working even in st st in Iris until top panel measures 5[8:12]in (13[20.5:30.5]cm) ending on a WS row.
Adjust length here if required.
Dec as follows:
Row 1: K2tog, K to last 2 sts, K2tog.
Row 2: P2tog, P to last 2 sts, P2tog.
Rep these two rows until 22[34:56] sts.

Cont in st st until top piece measures 8[11:15]in (20.5[28:38]cm) ending on a WS row.
Leave rem st on a stitch holder.

Under Panel (bottom upwards)

Using Iris and 4mm (US 6) needles, CO 16[22:28] sts.
Work in st st until work measures 4.5[7:10]in (11.5[28:38]cm ending on a WS row.
Adjust length here if required.
Dec 1 st at each end of next and every foll row until 10 sts rem.
Work even in st st until under panel measures 5[8:12]in (13[20.5:30.5]cm ending on a WS row.
Leave rem sts on a stitch holder.

Collar

With RS facing and using Elle Plume and 4mm (US 6) needles, PUK 26[36:44] sts across the neck edge of top panel and then K across the sts on the stitch holder of the under panel. The two pieces should be sitting side by side on one needle, 36[46:54] sts in total. Work even in garter st until neck measures 1[1.5:2]in (2.5[4:5]cm) ending on a WS row and then cast off loosely.

Knitted in cute pastels and edged in fur and frills, your best pal will feel warm and loved every time she wears it.

Interim Making Up

Tidy up loose yarn ends then with RS facing, pin and sew neck and side seams leaving 2[2.5:3]in (5[6.5:8]cm) gaps on each side for the leg openings, 3[4:5]in (8[10:13]cm) down from beneath the collar seam.

Bottom Frill

With RS facing, and using either 5dpns or circular needle and Iris, PUK 16[22:28] sts across edge of under panel, 22 sts along left-side edge, 22[34:56] sts from st holder, 22 sts down right-side edge. 82[100:128] sts in total.
Round 1: Change to Hollyhock and P this round.
Round 2: Change back to Iris and K into front and back of every st, 164[200:256] sts in total.
Now K every round until frill measures 1in (2.5cm).
Next Round: P.
Cast off purlwise.

Legs

Using dpns and Iris, PUK 24[30:34] sts around leg opening.
Round 1: Change to Hollyhock and P.
Round 2: Change back to Iris and K.
Round 3: P.
Cast off purlwise.
Rep for other leg.

Finishing

Darn in all loose yarn ends and press lightly.

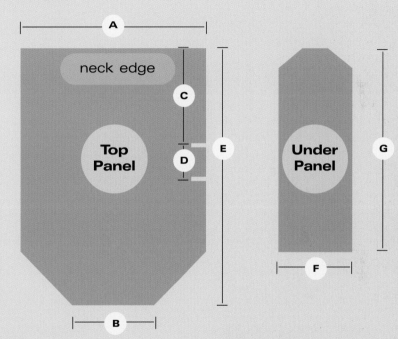

Top Panel

A 7[11:14]in (18[28:35.5]cm)

B 4[6:10]in (10[15.5:25.5]cm)

C 3[4:5]in (8[10:13]cm)

D 2[2.5:3]in (5[6.5:8]cm)

E 9[12:16]in (23[30.5:41]cm)

Under Panel

F 3[4:5]in (8[10:13]cm)

G 5[8:12]in (13[20.5:30.5]cm)

Fetch!

Go to page 14 to see more pictures

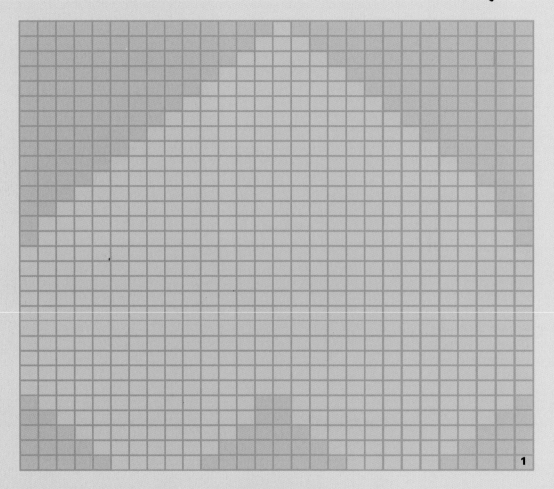

1

Heart Chart
28 sts x 30 rows
Work from right to left on RS rows and left to right on WS rows

Macho Males

Park Life

I've designed this casual striped hoodie in autumnal fruit pie colours but you could choose any colourway that appeals.

Materials and Equipment

- Patons Diploma Gold in:
  Apple Green,
  2[2:2:3] x 1¾oz (50g) balls
  Cream,
  1[1:2:2] x 1¾oz (50g) balls
  Iris,
  1[1:2:2] x 1¾oz (50g) balls
  Lupin,
  1[1:2:2] x 1¾oz (50g) balls
- 4mm (US 6) and 3.75mm (US 5) needles
- 5 x 3.75mm (US 5) dpns
- 2 brass eyelets, plus tool

Tension

22 sts and 30 rows over 4in (10cm)

Sizing

S[M:L:XL]
Chest: 14[18:22:26]in
(35.5[46:56:66]cm)
Actual: 16[20:25:29]in
(41[51:63.5:74]cm)
Length: 10[14:18:20]in
(25.5[35.5:46:51]cm)

Top Panel

Using Apple Green and 3.75mm (US 5) needles CO 60[76:96:112] sts
**Row 1: * K2, P2 * rep from * to * to end.
Rep this rib row 5 more times (6 rows in total) and then change

to 4mm (US 6) needles and Cream. Starting with a knit row, begin stripe patt in stocking stitch as follows:
Cream – 6 rows st st.
Iris – 6 rows st st.
Lupin – 6 rows st st.
Apple Green – 6 rows st st.
These 24 rows form the stripe sequence.**
Rep until work measures 10[14:18:20]in

(25.5[35.5:46:51]cm) ending on a WS row.
Adjust length here if required.
Dec for neck as follows:
Row 1: K15[12:19:13] * K2tog* rep from * to * to last 15[12:19:13] sts, K to end.
Row 2: P. Cast off in garter st.

Under Panel

Using Apple Green and 3.75mm (US 5) needles CO 30[36:40:52] sts.
Work as for top panel from ** to **.
Cont in stripe patt until under panel measures 10 rows less than top panel ending on a WS row.

Divide for Neck

Keeping to stripe patt:
Row 1: K2tog at beg and end of row, 28[34:38:50] sts.
Row 2: P2tog at beg and end of row, 26[32:36:48] sts.
Row 3: K2tog, K11[14:16:22] sts. Turn.
Row 4: Working on these sts only, P to last 2 sts, P2tog.
Row 5: K2tog, K9[12:14:20] sts. Turn.
Row 6: P to last 2 sts, P2tog.
Row 7: K2tog, K7[10:12:18] sts, Turn.
Row 8: P to last 2 sts, P2tog.
Row 9: K2tog, K5[8:10:16] sts,

Turn.

Row 10: P.

Cast off rem 6[9:11:17] sts.

Rejoin yarn to left-hand side of neck and rep rows 2–10 working the shapings in reverse.

Hood

Using Apple Green and 4mm (US 6) needles CO 55[65:87:97] sts.

Keeping the stripe patt throughout the hood,

Row 1: K.

Row 2: P.

Row 3: K10[20:32:36] sts, inc into next 25 sts, K10[20:31:36] sts, 70[90:111:122] sts in total.

Keeping the stripe patt, work in st st until hood measures 4[4.5:5:5.5]in (10[11.5:13:14.5]cm) ending on a WS row.

Dec as follows:

Row 1: K33[43:53:59], ssk, K2tog, K33[43:54:59].

Row 2: P32[42:52:58], P2tog twice, P32[42:53:58].

Row 3: K31[41:51:57], ssk, K2tog, K31[41:52:57].

Row 4: P30[40:50:56] P2tog twice, P30[40:51:56].

Cont dec as set until 56[66:88:98] sts remain.

Work even in stripe patt until hood measures 6.5[7:7.5:8]in (16.5[18:19:20.5]cm) ending on a WS row.

Cast off in garter stitch.

With RS facing, fold hood in half lengthways, sew centre top seam.

Interim Making Up

Tidy yarn ends and with RS facing, sew top and under panel pieces together, leaving 2.5[3:3.5:3.5]in (6.5[8:9:9]cm) openings on either side for leg holes, 4[5:7:8]in (10[13:18:20.5]cm) down from neck edge.

Sew hood in place.

Legs

With RS facing and using Apple Green and four 3.75mm (US 5) dpns, PUK 32[36:40:40] sts around leg opening.

**Row 1: * K2, P2 * rep from * to * to end. Rep this rib row 5 more times. (6 rows in total).

Cast off loosely in rib. **

Rep for other leg.

Hood Edging

With RS facing and using Apple Green and five 3.75mm (US 5) dpns, PUK 80[80:96:96] sts around the hood opening.

Rep as for leg edging from ** to **.

Sew in loose yarn ends, then tuck the bottom of the rib bands underneath each other where they meet the split in the under panel.

Pin and sew neatly into place.

Final Details

Tidy up any remaining yarn ends. Now, using the tool, insert two brass eyelets. You need to position them either side of the rib bands of the hood, just below the neck edge of the under panel. Finally, make two 2in (5cm) pompoms (see 'Knitting Essentials', page 130, if you're not sure how to tackle this) in any colour you like. I've used all the colours but you could just use one or two. Attach the pompoms to 3in (8cm) twisted or plaited cords then thread through each eyelet and make a knot to secure them.

Fetch! Go to page 15 to see more pictures

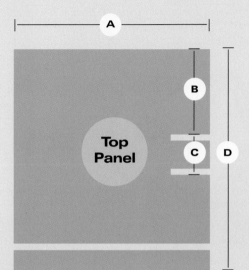

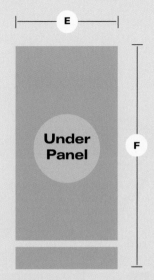

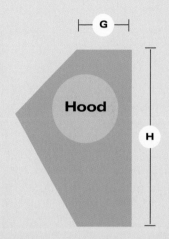

Top Panel

A 11[14:18:20]in
(28[35.5:46:51]cm)

B 4[5:7:8]in
(10[13:18:20.5]cm)

C 2.5[3:3.5:3.5]in
(6.5[8:9:9]cm)

D 10[14:18:20]in
(25.5[35.5:46:51]cm)

Under Panel

E 5[6:7:9]in
(13[15.5:18:23]cm)

F 10[14:18:20]in
(25.5[35.5:46:51]cm)

Hood

G 5[6:8:9]in
(13[15.5:20.5:23]cm)

H 6.5[7:7.5:8]in
(16.5[18:19:20.5]cm)

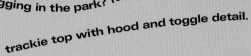

Keeping an eye on your figure? Jogging in the park? Now your dog can come too in this sporty trackie top with hood and toggle detail.

Materials and Equipment
- Patons 100% DK Cotton in: Indigo, 2[2:3:4] x 3½oz (100g) balls
  White, 1 x 3½oz (100g) ball
- 4mm (US 6) and 3.75mm (US 5) needles
- 5 x 3.75mm (US 5) dpns
- Navy cord, 19½in (50cm)
- 2 plastic toggles
- 2 brass eyelets, plus tool

Tension
22 sts x 30 rows over 4in (10cm)

Sizing
S[M:L:XL]
Chest: 14[18:22:26]in (35.5[46:56:66]cm)
Actual: 16[20:25:29]in (41[51:63.5:74]cm)
Length: 10[14:18:20]in (25.5[35.5:46:51]cm)

Top Panel (bottom upwards)
Using 3.75mm (US 5) needles and Indigo CO 60[76:98:110] sts.
**Row 1: * K1, P1 * rep from * to * to end.
Row 2: As row 1. Change to White.
Rows 3–4: As row 1. Change to Indigo.
Rows 5–6: As row 1. Change to White.

Rows 7–8: As row 1. Change to Indigo.
Rows 9–10: As row 1. Change to 4mm (US 6) needles and work in st st until work measures 10[14:18:20]in (25.5[35.5:46:51]cm) ending on a WS row. *Adjust length here if required.*
Dec for neck as follows:
Row 1: K15[12:19:13], *K2tog * rep from * to * to last 15[12:19:13] sts,

K to end, 45[50:68:68] sts in total.
Row 2: P.
Cast off knitwise.

Under Panel
Using 3.75mm (US 5) needles and Indigo CO 28[34:38:50] sts and rep as for top panel from ** to ** but ending 10 rows shorter.

Divide for Neck
Still working in st st:
Row 1: K2tog at beg and end of row 26[32:36:48] sts.
Row 2: P2tog at beg and end of row 24[30:34:46] sts.
Row 3: K2tog, K10[13:15:21] sts, Turn.
Row 4: Working on these sts only, P to last 2 sts, K2tog.
Row 5: K2tog, K8[11:13:18].
Row 6: P to last 2 sts, P2tog.
Row 7: K2tog, K6[9:11:16].
Row 8: P to last 2 sts, P2tog.
Row 9: K2tog, K4[7:14].
Row 10: P.
Cast off these 5[8:10:15] sts.
Rejoin yarn to left-hand side of neck and rep from rows 3–10, reversing shapings.

Hood
Using Indigo and 4mm (US 6) needles CO 55[65:87:97] sts.
Row 1: K.
Row 2: P.

Of course, tracksuits are great for chilling, too, so after your run, why not slip this cool sweater over your best pal's head, load up your favourite CD and crash on the sofa together with a glass of something cool.

Row 2: P.

Row 3: K10[20:31:36], inc into next 25 sts, K10[20:31:36]. 70[90:111:122] sts in total. Work even in st st until hood measures 4[4.5:5:5.5]in (10[11.5:13:14.5]cm) ending on a WS row.

Dec as follows:

Row 1: K33[43:53:59], ssk, K2tog, K33[43:54:59].

Row 2: P32[42:52:58], P2tog twice, P32[42:53:58].

Row 3: K31[41:52:57], ssk, K2tog, K31[41:52:57].

Row 4: P30[40:50:56], P2tog twice, P30[40:51:56].

Cont dec as set until 56[66:88:98] sts rem.

Work even in st st until hood measures 6.5[7:7.5:8]in (16.5[18:19:20.5]cm) ending on a WS row and then cast off.

With RS facing, fold the hood in half lengthways then sew up the top centre seam.

Pocket

Using 4mm (US 6) needles and Indigo CO 44 sts.

Work in st st for 2in (5cm) ending on a WS row.

Dec as follows:

Row 1: K2, ssk, K to last 4 sts, K2tog, K2.

Row 2: P2, P2tog, p to last 4 sts, P2tog, P2.

Rep these last 2 rows until 16 sts rem ending on a WS row.

Work in st st until pocket measures 4in (10cm) and then cast off.

Interim Making Up

Press pieces lightly. Now, with RS facing, pin and sew the top and under panel pieces together, making sure to leave 2.5[3:3.5:3.5]in (6.5[8:9:9]cm) openings on each side for leg holes, 4[5:7:8]in (10[13:18:20.5]cm) down from the neck edge.

Pin and sew the pocket to the top piece. Position it centrally and slightly up from the bottom rib. Pin and sew the hood in place.

Legs

With RS facing and using 4dpns and Indigo, PUK 30[34:40:40] sts around the leg opening.

**Row 1: *K1, P1 * rep from * to * to end. Change to White.

Row 2: As row 1. Change to Indigo.

Rows 3–4: As row 1. Change to White.

Row 5: As row 1. Change to Indigo.

Row 6: As row 1.

Cast off loosely in rib.**

Rep for other leg.

Hood Edging

With RS facing and using 5dpns and Indigo, PUK 82[82:94:94] evenly around the edge of hood. Rep as for legs from ** to **.

Sew in loose yarn ends, then tuck the bottom of the rib bands underneath each other where they meet the split in the under panel. Pin and sew neatly into place.

Final Details

Tidy up any remaining yarn ends. Now, using the tool, insert two brass eyelets. You need to position them either side of the rib bands of the hood, just below the neck edge of the under panel. Once you have done that, cut two lengths of navy cord about 4in (10cm) in length. Thread a toggle onto the end of each cord before threading it carefully through the eyelet and tying a knot to secure.

Fetch!

Go to page 17 to see more pictures

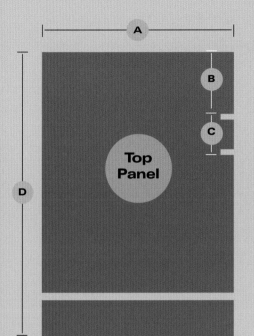

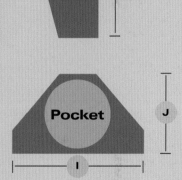

Top Panel

A 11[14:18:20]in
(28[35.5:46:51]cm)

B 4[5:7:8]in
(10[13:18:20.5]cm)

C 2.5[3:3.5:3.5]in
(6.5[8:9:9]cm)

D 10[14:18:20]in
(25.5[35.5:46:51]cm)

Under Panel

E 5[6:7:9]in
(13[15.5:18:23]cm)

F 10[14:18:20]in
(25.5[35.5:46:51]cm)

Hood

G 5[6:8:9]in
(13[15.5:20.5:23]cm)

H 6.5[7:7.5:8]in
(16.5[18:19:20.5]cm)

Pocket

I 8in (20.5cm)

J 4in (10cm)

Punk Vibe

Materials and Equipment

- Wendy DK with 25% wool in Grenadine, 1[1:2:2] x 3½oz (100g) balls
- Sunbeam Paris Mohair in Black, 1[2:2:3] x 1¾oz (50g) balls
- 4mm (US 6) needles
- 4 x 4mm (US 6) dpns
- 2 x stitch holders

Tension

22 sts and 30 rows to 4in (10cm)

Sizing

S[M:L:XL]

Chest: 14[18:22:26]in (35.5[46:56:66]cm)

Actual: 15[19:24:28]in (38[48.5:61:71]cm)

Length: 12[16:21:23]in (30.5[41:53.5:58.5]cm)

Top Panel *(bottom upwards)*

Using Black Mohair and 4mm needles CO 34[56:66:76] sts.

Row 1: * K1, P1 * rep from * to * to end.

Rep this rib row 3 more times (4 rows in total).

Beg stripe patt as follows:

Rows 1–4: Beg with a K row st st in Black.

Rows 5–8: Beg with a K row st st in Red.

At the same inc as follows:

Inc into first and last st of row 1

and every alt row until 60[76:94:98] sts.

Cont working in stripe patt until work measures 11[15:20:22]in (28[38:51:56]cm) ending on a WS row.

Adjust length here if required.

Dec for neck as follows:

K14[12:25:28], *K2tog * rep from * to * until last 14[12:25:28] sts, K to end, 44[50:72:82] sts in total.

Cont in strip patt until work measures 12[16:21:23]in (30.5[41:53.5:58.5]cm) ending on a Ws row.

Leave these rem sts on a holder.

Under Panel *(bottom upwards)*

Measure down from the neck of the top panel. Note the stripe colour at the 8[12:16:18]in (20.5[30.5:41:46]cm) point and beg the under panel with corresponding colour.

Using correct colour and 4mm (US 6) needles CO 22[28:34:44] sts.

Row 1: * K1, P1 * rep from * to * to end.

Rep this rib row 3 more times (4 rows in total).

Change colour and begin stripe patt as for top panel. Work even until under panel piece measures 2[3:3:5] stripes fewer than the top panel ending on a WS row.

Dec for neck as follows:

Keeping the stripe patt, K2tog at each end of next and every row until 10 sts remain.

Work even until piece matches the top panel in length ending on a WS row. Leave sts on a holder.

Neck

With RS facing and using black mohair and 4mm (US 6) needles, K across the 44[50:72:84] sts from the first holder and then the 10 sts of the second holder. The two pieces should sit side by side on one needle. 54[60:82:94] sts in total.

Row 1: * K1, P1 * rep from * to * to end.

Rep this rib row until neck measures 1[1.5:2:2.5]in (2.5[4:5:6.5]cm).

Cast off loosely in rib.

Interim Making Up

With RS facing, pin and sew neck and side seams leaving 2.5[3:3.5:3.5]in (6.5[8:9:9]cm) openings on each side for leg holes, 4[5:7:8]in (10[13:18:20.5]cm) from beneath the collar.

Legs

Using black mohair and 4 dpns PUK 28[34:38:38] sts around the leg opening.

Round 1: * K1, P1 * rep from * to * to end.

Rep round 1, 3 more times (4 rounds in total).

Cast off loosely in rib.

Rep for second leg.

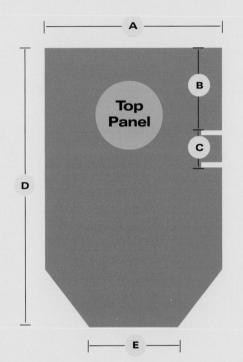

Top Panel

A 11[14:17:18]in (28[35.5:43.5:46]cm)

B 4[5:7:8]in (10[13:18:20.5]cm)

C 2.5[3:3.5:3.5]in (6.5[8:9:9]cm)

D 12[16:21:23]in (30.5[41:53.5:58.5]cm)

E 6[10:12:14]in (15.5[25.5:30.5:35.5]cm)

Under Panel

F 8[12:16:18]in (20.5[30.5:41:46]cm)

G 4[5:6:8]in (10[13:15.5:20.5]cm)

Fetch!

Go to page to see more pictures

Combat

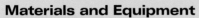

This manly sweater is ideal for the outdoor dog. Macho men everywhere will be happy to take their dog for a walk dressed in this khaki, ribbed army-style number.

Materials and Equipment

- Sirdar Country Style DK in Moss, 1[2:2:3] x 3½oz (100g) balls
- Jaeger Matchmaker DK in Shade 730 Loden, 1 x 1¾oz (50g) ball
- 4mm (US 6) needles
- 4 x 4mm (US 6) dpns
- Stitch holder

Tension

22 sts x 28 rows to 4in (10cm)

Sizing

S[M:L:XL]
Chest: 14[18:22:26]in (35.5[46:56:66]cm)
Actual: 15[19:24:28]in (38[48.5:61:71]cm)
Length: 12[16:21:23]in (30.5[41:53.5:58.5]cm)

Top Panel

Using Moss and 4mm (US 6) needles CO 60[76:96:100] sts.
Row 1: *K2, P2 * rep from * to * to end. Rep this rib row until top panel measures 12[16:21:23]in (30.5[41:53.5:58.5]cm) ending on a RS row.
Adjust length here if required.
Dec for neck as follows:
Patt 12[16:18:28] *K2tog * rep from * to * to last 12[16:18:28] sts. Patt to end.

42[54:66:78] sts in total.
Leave rem sts on a holder.

Under Panel

Using Moss and 4mm (US 6) needles CO 24[28:36:44] sts.
Rib as for top panel until piece measures 7[10.5:14:15.5]in (18[26.5:35.5:39.5]cm) ending on a WS row.
Adjust length here if required.
Next Row: Keeping patt. K2tog at each end of next and every foll row until 10 sts remain.
Work even in rib patt until under panel measures 8[12:16:18]in (20.5[30.5:41:46]cm) ending on a WS row.
Leave rem sts on a holder.

Neck

With RS facing, K across the stitch holder of the top panel and then the sts from the holder of the under panel. The two pieces should be sitting side by side on one needle, 52[64:76:88] sts in total.
Next Row: *K2, P2 * rep from * to * to end. Rep this rib row until neck measures 1[1.5:2:2.5]in (2.5[4:5:6.5]cm) and then cast off loosely in rib.

Interim Making Up

Tidy any loose yarn ends. With RS facing pin and sew neck and side seams leaving 2.5[3:3.5:3.5]in (6.5[8:9:9]cm) openings on either side for leg holes, 4[5:7:8]in (10[13:18:20.5]cm) down from under the neck.

Legs

Using Moss and 4dpns PUK 28[32:40:40] sts around the leg opening.
Row 1: *K2, P2 * rep from * to * until end of round.

Rep row 1 until leg measures 1[1.5:2:2.5]in (2.5[4:5:6.5]cm) and then cast off loosely in rib.
Rep for other leg.

Shoulder Patches – Make 2

Using Jaeger Matchmaker and 4mm (US 6) needles CO 12[18:20:22] sts.
Row 1: K.
Row 2: K1, P10[16:18:20], K1.
Rep these 2 rows until the shoulder patches measure 2[3:3.5:4]in (5[8:9:10]cm) ending on a WS row.
Cast off.

Finishing

Tidy any loose yarn ends and then pin and sew the shoulder patches in place. Position them at the shoulder line, just below the neckband and above the leg openings. If you are not sure, then try the sweater on your dog first and pin in place while he's wearing it.

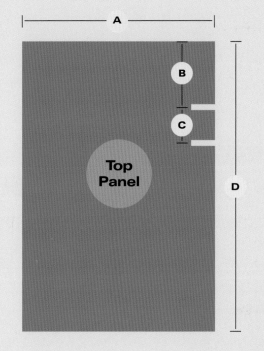

Top Panel

Under Panel

Top Panel

A 11[14:17:18]in
(28[35.5:43.5:46]cm)

B 4[5:7:8]in
(10[13:18:20.5]cm)

C 2.5[3:3.5:3.5]in
(6.5[8:9:9]cm)

D 12[16:21:23]in
(30.5[41:53.5:58.5]cm)

Under Panel

E 8[12:16:18]in
(20.5[30.5:41:46]cm)

F 4[5:6:8]in
(10[13:15.5:20.5]cm)

Fetch! Go to page 16 to see more pictures

Mod Parka

This fun dog jacket takes inspiration from Jimmy in the film Quadrophenia.

Materials and Equipment

- Stylecraft Aran with wool in Moss, 1 x 14oz (400g) ball
- Elle Sensual in Candle Light Shade 262, 1 x 1¾oz (50g) ball
- 5mm (US 8) needles
- 4 x 5mm (US 8) dpns
- 4mm (US G/6) crochet hook
- 6[8:10:11] jeans buttons, plus tool
- Buff cording, 6½ft (2m)
- 2 anorak toggles

Tension

18 sts x 24 rows over 4in (10cm)

Sizing

S[M:L:XL]
Chest: 14[18:22:26]in (35.5[46:56:66]cm)
Actual: 17[21:26:30]in (43.5[53.5:66:76.5]cm)
Length: 12[17:23:26]in (30.5[43.5:58.5:66]cm)

Main Body (neck to bottom)

Using Aran Moss and 5mm (US 8) needles CO 46[54:64:72] sts.
Row 1: K.
Row 2: K4, P to last 4 sts, K4.
These two rows set the patt.
Rep once more.
Inc for shoulders as follows:
Next Row: K8[7:6:5], inc into every

st until last 8[7:6:5] sts. K to end. 75[94:116:134] sts in total.
Next Row: As row 2.
Next Row (buttonhole row): K2, YO, K2tog, K to end.
Next Row: As row 2.
Cont to work in patt rows 1 and 2 until work measures 4[5:7:8]in

(10[13:18:20.5]cm) ending on a WS row.
At the same time, remember to work the buttonhole row at the 3, 5 and 7in (8[13:18]cm) points where applicable.

Divide for Legs

Next Row: K16[18:20:22], start a new ball of yarn, K44[58:76:90], start a new ball of yarn, K16[18:20:22]
Working separately on these three sections, cont in patt rows 1 and 2 as before for 2.5[3:3.5:3.5]in (6.5[8:9:9]cm) ending on a WS row.
At the same time, remember to work buttonhole rows at the 5, 7, 9 and 11in (13[18:23:28]cm) points where applicable.
Next Row: Work straight across all three sections with one ball of yarn.
Next Row: As row 2.
Now work even until piece measures 8[10:14:16]in (20.5[25.5:35.5:41]cm) ending on a WS row.
At the same time, remember to work buttonhole rows at the 7, 9, 11 13, 15in (18[23:28:38]cm) points where applicable.

With cute fishtails and fur-lined hood detailing, all you need to set the scene is a Lambretta scooter and an old eight-track blasting out the sounds of the Sixties.

Cord Casing

Next Row (RS): P.
Next Row: P.
Next Row: K2, YO, K2tog, K to last 4 sts, K2tog, YO, K2.
Next 2 rows: P.
Next 4 rows: st st, beg with a K row and then cast off.
Tidy up loose yarn ends. Fold and pin the cord casing up inside the WS of the jacket body. The K row should sit at the bottom edge. Slip stitch neatly into place.

Fishtails Left Side

Using Aran Moss and 5mm (US 8) needles CO 42[52:62:72] sts
Row 1: K.
Row 2: K4, P to last 4 sts, K4
Rep these rows twice more.
Next Row (buttonhole row): K2, YO, K2 tog, K to last 4 sts, K2tog, YO, K2.
Next Row: As row 2.
Rep rows 1 and 2 until work measures 2in (5cm) ending on a row 2.
Next Row: Cast off 21[26:31:36] sts, K to end.
Next Row: K4, P to end.

Dec for tail as follows:
Next Row: K2tog, K to end.
Next Row: K4, P to last 2 sts, P2tog.
Rep these last two rows until work measures 3in (8cm) ending on a row 2.
Next Row: K2tog, K to last 4 sts, K2tog, YO, K2.
Next Row: K4, P to last 2 sts, P2tog.
Now rep the two dec rows as before until 2 sts remain.
Next Row: K2tog and fasten off.

Fishtails Right Side

Using Aran Moss and 5mm (US 8) needles CO 42[52:62:72] sts
Row 1: K.
Row 2: K4, P to last 4 sts, K4.
Rep for 2in (5cm) ending on a row 1.
Next Row: Cast off 21[26:31:36] sts, P to last 4 sts, K4.
Next Row: K.
Dec for tail as follows:
Row 1: P2tog, P to last 4 sts, K4.
Row 2: K to last 2 sts, K2tog.
Rep these 2 dec rows until 2 sts remain.

Next Row: K2tog.
Fasten off.

Finishing

With RS facing and using Aran Moss and 5mm (US 8) needles, PUK 20[26:31:36] sts along straight bottom edge and 20[24:32:36] sts down the tail edge. 40[50:63:72] sts in total.
Next Row: P.
Next Row: Cast off in garter st.
Rep for second fishtail.
Tidy any loose yarn ends and pin each fishtail carefully along lower edge of cord casing of main jacket body. Remember to overlap the button bands at the centre back of jacket. Slip stitch neatly in place. Press lightly into shape.

Fetch!

Go to page 14 to see more pictures

Hood

Using Aran Moss and 5mm (US 8) needles CO 45[53:63:71] sts.

Row 1: K.

Row 2: K2, P to last 2 sts, K2.

Row 3: K10[14:19:23], inc into next 25 sts, K10[14:19:23], (70[78:88:96] sts in total.

Row 4: K2, P to last 2 sts, K2.

Rep rows 1 and 2 until hood measures 4[4.5:5:5.5]in (10[11.5:13:14.5]cm) ending on a row 2.

Dec as follows:

Row 1: K33[37:42:46], skpo, K2tog, K33[37:42:46].

Row 2: K2, P30[34:39:43], P2tog twice, P30[34:39:43], K2.

Row 3: K31[35:40:44], skpo, K2tog, K31[35:40:44].

Row 4: K2, P28[32:37:41], P2tog twice, P28[32:37:41], K2.

Rep decreases as set until 46[54:64:72] sts remain.

Work even in patt rows 1 and 2 as before until work measures 6.5[7:7.5:8]in (16.5[18:19:20.5]cm) ending on row 2. Cast off.

Now fold hood in half with RS facing and pin and sew centre top seam.

Finishing

With RS facing, and using a 4mm (US 6) crochet hook and Elle Sensual, work 1 row of dc evenly around the front edge of hood.

Row 2: Make a ch, turn and work a second row of dc.

Fasten off and tidy loose yarn ends. Using the end of a knitting needle, gently tease out the strands of fur so that it fluffs out nicely around the hood.

Pin the hood onto the jacket body and slip stitch neatly into place.

Legs

With RS facing, using Aran Moss and 4 x 5mm (US 8) dpns, PUK 24[28:32:32] sts around leg opening.

Garter st every round until leg measures 1[1.5:2:2.5]in (2.5[4:5:6.5]cm).

Next 2 Rounds: P.

Cast off loosely.

Rep for other leg then tidy loose yarn ends.

Final Finishing

Using the special tool included in the pack, line up and punch the jean buttons in place down the front of the jacket and also on the fishtails. Thread the cord through the waist casing and cut to length. Thread toggles onto each end and knot the ends to prevent the cord from fraying.

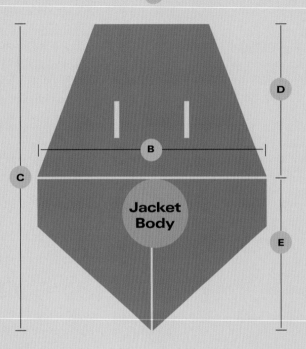

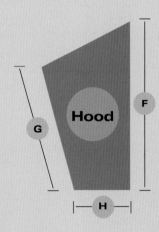

Jacket Body

A 10[12:14:16]in
(25.5[30.5:35.5:41]cm)

B 17[21:26:30]in
(43.5[53.5:66:76.5]cm)

C 12[17:23:26]in
(30.5[43.5:58.5:66]cm)

D 8[10:14:16]cm
(20.5[25.5:35.5:41]cm)

E 4[7:9:10]in
(10[18:23:25.5]cm)

Hood

F 6.5[7:7.5:8]in
(16.5[18:19:20.5]cm)

G 4[4.5:5:5.5]in
(10[11.5:13:14.5]cm)

H 5[6:7:8]in
(13[15.5:18:20.5]cm)

Diamond Guy

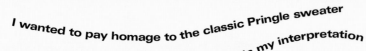
I wanted to pay homage to the classic Pringle sweater and so here is my interpretation of it for your pet pooch.

Materials and Equipment

🐾 Sirdar Luxury Soft Cotton in French Navy,
2[2:3:4] x 1¾oz (50g) balls
Vanilla Cream,
1[1:2:2] x 1¾oz (50g) balls
Ruby Red,
1[1:2:2] x 1¾oz (50g) balls
🐾 3.75mm (US 5) and 4mm (US 6) needles
🐾 4 x 3.75mm (US 5) dpns
🐾 2 x stitch holders

Tension

22 sts x 28 rows over
4in (10cm)

Sizing

S[M:L:XL]
Chest: 14[18:22:26]in
(35.5[46:56:66]cm)
Actual: 16[20:25:29)in
(41[51:63.5:74]cm)
Length: 10[14:18:20]in
(25.5[35.5:46:51]cm)

Top Panel

Using French Navy and 3.75mm (US 5) needles CO 60[76:96:110] sts.
Row 1: *K1, P1 * rep from * to * to end. Rep this rib row for 1[1:2:2]in (2.5[2.5:5:5]cm) ending on a WS row. Change to 4mm (US 6) needles.
Beg the intarsia chart on page 70 as follows:

Row 1: K11[19:29:26] sts, work 38 sts on first row of chart, K11[19:29:26].
Row 2: P11[19:29:26] sts, work 38 sts on second row of chart, P11[19:29:26].
Cont as set, alternating the colours of the diamonds as you go, until work measures 10[14:18:20]in (25.5[35.5:46:51]cm) ending on a WS row.
Adjust length here if required.
Change to French Navy.

Dec for neck as follows:
K12[16:18:23], * K2tog * rep from * to * until last 12[16:18:23] sts, K to end. 42[54:66:78] sts in total.
Next Row: P.
Leave rem sts on a stitch holder.

Under Panel

Using French Navy and 3.75mm (US 5) needles, CO 28[34:38:50] sts.
Work as for top panel from ** to **
Cont in st st until work measures 9[12:16:17]in (23[30.5:41:43.5]cm) ending on a WS row.
Adjust length here if required.
Dec for neck as follows:
Row 1: K2tog, K to last 2 sts, K2tog 26[32:36:48] sts.
Row 2: P2tog, P to last 2 sts, P2tog 24[30:34:46] sts.
Rep these two decreasing rows until 10 sts rem.
Work in st st until under panel measures 10[14:18:20]in. (25.5[35.5:46:51]cm) ending on a WS row.
Leave rem sts on a stitch holder.

Neck

With RS facing, using French Navy and 3.75mm (US 5) needles, K across the stitch holder of the top panel. Then, K across the 10 sts of the under panel. The 2 pieces should be sitting side by side on one needle, 52[64:76:88] sts in total.

Row 1: * K1, P1 * rep from * to *
to end.
Rep this rib row until neck
measures 1[1:2:2]in
(2.5[2.5:5:5]cm), ending on
a WS row.
Cast off loosely in rib.

Interim Making Up

Tidy loose yarn ends and pin and
sew neck and side seams leaving
2.5[3:3.5:3.5]in (6.5[8:9:9]cm)
openings on either side, 4[5:7:8]in
(10[13:18:20.5]cm) down from
beneath the neckband for leg holes.

Legs

With RS facing, using French Navy
and four 3.75mm (US 5) dpns,
PUK 28[32:40:40] sts around the
leg openings.
Round 1: * K1, P1 * rep from * to *
to end.
Rep this rib round until leg bands
measure 1[1:2:2]in
(2.5[2.5:5:5]cm), ending on a
WS row.
Cast off loosely in rib.

Finishing

Tidy up loose yarn ends and then
press lightly.

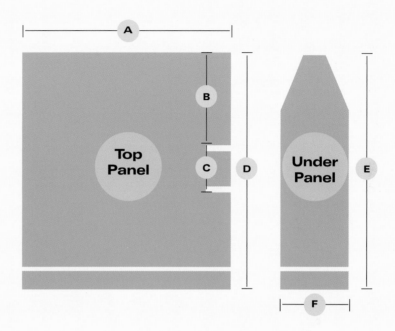

Top Panel

A   11[14:18:20]in
(28[35.5:46:51]cm)

B   4[5:7:8]in
(10[13:18:20.5]cm)

C   2.5[3:3.5:3.5]in
(6.5[8:9:9]cm)

D   10[14:18:20]in
(25.5[35.5:46:51]cm)

Under Panel

E   10[14:18:20]in
(25.5[35.5:46:51]cm)

F   5[6:7:9]in
(13[15.5:18:23]cm)

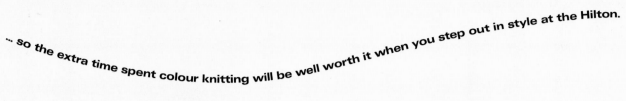

... so the extra time spent colour knitting will be well worth it when you step out in style at the Hilton.

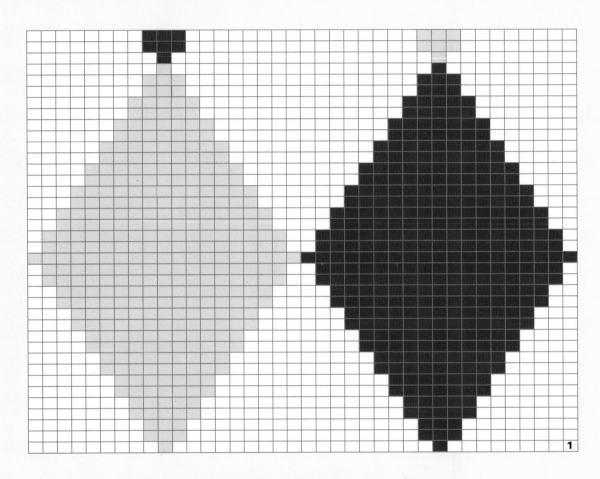

Diamond Guy Chart
38 sts x 35 rows

Fetch!
Go to page **17** to see more pictures

Fair Isle

This classic style of jumper is much favoured by urban and country dwellers alike.

Materials and Equipment

* Stylecraft Pure Wool DK in:
  Navy, 1[2:2] x 3½oz
  (100g) balls
  Cascade, 1[1:2] x 3½oz
  (100g) balls
  Cream, 1[1:2] x 3½oz
  (100g) balls
* 4mm (US 6) and 3.75mm
  (US 5) needles
* 5 x 3.75 (US 5) dpns
* Stitch holder

Tension

22 sts x 30 rows over
4in (10cm)

Sizing

S[M:L]
Chest: 14[18:22]in
(35.5:46:56]cm)
Actual: 16[20:25]in
(41[51:63.5]cm)
Length: 10[14:18]in
(25.5[35.5:46]cm)

Top Panel

Using Navy and 3.75mm (US 5)
needles CO 65[75:95] sts.
Row 1: * K1, P1 * rep from * to *
to end.
Row 2: * P1, K1, * rep from * to *
to end. Rep these 2 rib rows for
1in (2.5cm) ending on a row 2.
Change to 4mm (US 6) needles.
Using st st, begin working from

the Fair Isle chart (page 74). Read
RS rows from right to left and WS
rows from left to right. There are
only 2 colours maximum per row.
Carry the colours across the row
using the stranding method (check
'Knitting Essentials', page 128, if
you are unsure). ** Work in patt
until work measures 10[14:18]in
(25.5[35.5:46]cm), ending on a
WS row.
Adjust length here if required.
Dec for neck as follows:
Next Row: K3[1:1] *K2tog * rep
from * to * to end, 34[38:48] sts
in total.

Next Row: P.
Leave rem sts on a stitch holder.

Under Panel

Using Navy and 3.75mm (US 5)
needles CO 30[35:45]. Work as for
front from ** to ** until work
measures 7[11:14]in
(18[28:35.5]cm) ending on a WS
row. *Adjust length here if required.*

Divide for Neck

Still keeping to chart:
Row 1: Patt 15[17:22], turn. Leave
rem 15[18:23] sts on holder.
Row 2: P2tog, patt to end.
14[16:21] sts.
Row 3: Patt.
Rep rows 2 and 3 until 5[5:7] sts
rem. Work in patt until under panel
matches top ending on a WS row.
Cast off.
With RS facing rejoin yarn to left-
hand side of neck.
Row 1: K2tog, patt to end of row
14[17:22] sts.
Row 2: Patt.
Rep these two rows until 5[5:7]
sts rem. Work in patt until under
panel matches top ending on WS
row then cast off.

Interim Making Up

Tidy all loose yarn ends and press
lightly. Pin and sew side seams
leaving 2.5[3:3.5]in (6.5[8:9]cm)

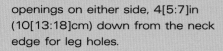

Wear a matching one alongside your dog, topped with an oversized beanie hat for that Michael Stipe/REM feel or with a wax jacket and walking boots for a country weekend outing.

openings on either side, 4[5:7]in (10[13:18]cm) down from the neck edge for leg holes.

Legs

With RS facing, using four 3.75mm (US 5) dpns and Navy, PUK 28[34:38] sts around leg opening.
Round 1: *K1, P1 * rep from * to * to end.
Rep round 1 for 6 rounds and then cast off loosely in rib.
Rep for other leg.

Neckband

With RS facing, using five 3.75mm (US 5) dpns and Navy, PUK 28 sts up right front 'V', knit across the 34[38:48] sts from st holder and PUK 28 sts down the left front 'V'. 90[94:104] sts in total.
Row 1: * K1, P1 * rep from * to * to end.
Rep this rib row, working back and forward along the row (i.e. do not work as a round) for 6 rows.
Cast off loosely in rib.

Finishing

Tidy loose yarns. Tuck one edge of neckband neatly behind the other at the point of the front 'V'. Finally, secure neatly to front opening with a few small stitches.

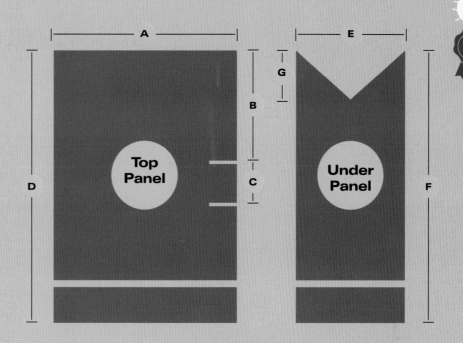

Top Panel

A   11[14:17]in 28[35.5:43.5]cm)

B   4[5:7]in (10[13:18]cm)

C   2.5[3:3.5]in (6.5[8:9]cm)

D   10[14:18]in (25.5[35.5:46]cm)

Under Panel

E   5[6:8]in (13[15.5:20.5]cm)

F   10[14:18]in (25.5[35.5:46]cm)

G   4in (10cm)

Fetch!
Go to page  **16** to see more pictures

This sweater will never date and your dog will love you for knitting it for him.

Fair Ilse Chart
10 sts x 32 rows repeat

That's enough of clothes, what about some toys and accessories?

Turn over to find new ways for your pet to have fun!

Accessories

For All

Fur Bone

**Princess
Pussycat Throne**

Fur Bone

Knits for dogs and cats

Fetch!

Follow Mutley's paw prints to see each project

114 **Kitten Mitten**
Moody Blue

114 **Kitten Mitten**
Dear Heart

102

Shoe Chew

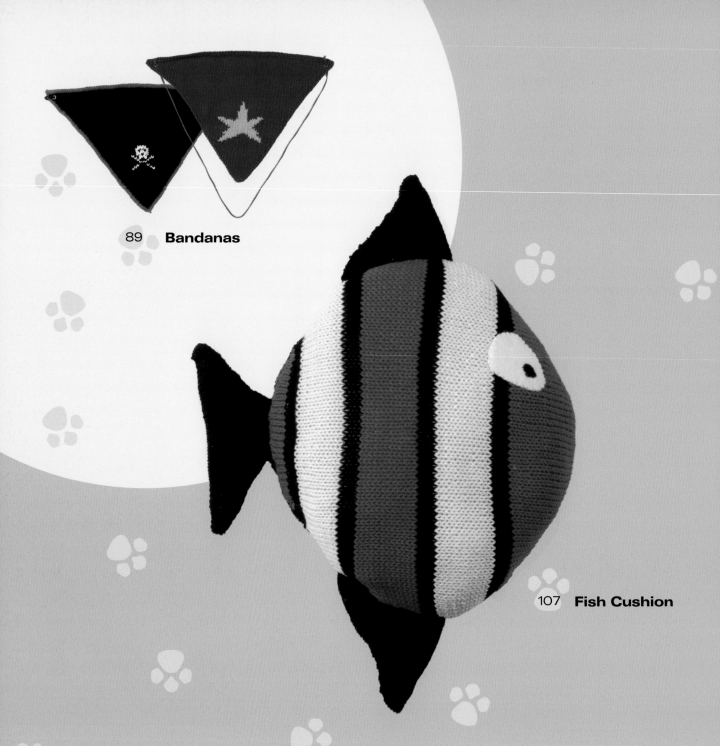

89 Bandanas

107 Fish Cushion

83

Doggy Bag

98 **Dog Tired/Cat Nap**

96 **Cable Twist Scarf**

For Cats
and Dogs

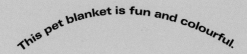
This pet blanket is fun and colourful.

Materials and Equipment

- Patons 100% Cotton DK in:
  Cream, shade 02692,
  3 x 3$\frac{1}{2}$oz (100g) balls
  Denim, shade 02697,
  3 x 3$\frac{1}{2}$oz (100g) balls
  Foxglove, shade 02706,
  3 x 3$\frac{1}{2}$oz (100g) balls
  Nougat, shade 02715,
  1 x 3$\frac{1}{2}$oz (100g) ball
  Black, shade 02712,
  1 x 3$\frac{1}{2}$oz (100g) ball
- 4mm (US 6) needles
- One pair of 4mm (US 6)
  circular needles, 39in (100cm)
  in length

Tension

22 sts x 30 rows over 4in (10cm)

Sizing

There are a total of 25 squares in
this blanket. Each square measures
6 x 6in (15 x 15cm).
The completed blanket measures
30 x 30in (70 x 70cm) plus border.

Two-colour Stripe

You will need six of these squares.
Three squares are worked in
Foxglove/Cream and three squares
in Denim/Cream.
Using MC (either Foxglove or
Denim) and 4mm (US 6) needles
CO 36 sts.

I've used a combination
of stripes, textures
and motifs that you

can mix up

and experiment with

any way you like.

Working in st st and beginning
with a K row cont in stripe patt as
follows:
Rows 1–3: MC.
Rows 4–6: Cream.
Rep these 6 rows for 45 rows or
6in (15cm) and cast off.

Multi Stripe

You will need three of these
squares. Using 4mm (US 6)
needles and Cream CO 36 sts.
Work stripe patt in st st as follows
beginning with a purl row.
Rows 1–3: Cream.
Rows 4–6: Denim.
Rows 7–9: Cream.
Rows 10–13: Foxglove.
Rep these 13 rows for 45 rows or
6in (15cm) and cast off.

Texture

You will need a total of 12 of
these squares: four in Denim, four
in Cream and four in Foxglove.
Using chosen colour and 4mm
(US 6) needles CO 37 sts.
Row 1: K.
Row 2: K1, * P1, K1* rep to * to
last st, K1.
Row 3: K.
Row 4: K2 *P1, K1 * rep from *
to * to end.
Rep these four rows until square
measures 6in (15cm).
Cast off.

Picture Squares

You will need four of these in total.
You can choose either to knit all of
the dog/cat motifs or to work two
of each.

Whether you knit the dog motifs or just cat squares, or choose to mingle them as I have, you're sure to come up with a combination that's unique to you and your pet.

Dog Squares

Using Foxglove and 4mm (US 6) needles CO 36 sts.
Starting with a K row, work 6 rows in st st ending on a WS row. Begin intarsia chart on page 87 as follows:
Row 1: K5, work first row of chart, K6.
Row 2: P6, work second row of chart, P5.
Cont as set until chart is complete. Change to Foxglove and work five more rows of st st.
Cast off.

Cat Squares

Using Denim and 4mm (US 6) needles CO 36 sts.
Starting with a K row, work 8 rows in st st ending on a WS row. Begin intarsia chart on page 86 as follows:
Row 1: K6, work first row of chart, K7.
Row 2: P7, work second row of chart, P6.
Cont as set until chart is complete. Change to Denim and work 8 more rows of st st.
Cast off.
Backstitch whiskers and mouth with a length of black yarn.

Making Up

Now the hard bit is over you don't want to ruin your blanket in the making-up process. First tidy up and weave in any loose ends then lightly press each square to size and shape under a damp cloth. Arrange them on a flat surface and experiment with various combinations until you're satisfied. Begin sewing them together in vertical columns using mattress stitch. Ease the squares gently into place along the seam if they don't quite match. Now sew up each column and press the whole item again lightly under a damp cloth.

Edging

Work each of the four sides separately as follows:
Using 4mm (US 5) circular needles and Cream PUK 150 sts along first edge. Working in garter st, inc 1 st into first and last st of next and every following row. Proceed in stripe patt as follows:
Rows 1–3: Cream.
Rows 4–5: Denim.
Rows 6–7: Foxglove.
Cast off loosely in garter st.
Rep for other three sides.
Finally, weave in any loose ends and sew mitred corners neatly together. Give it all a final press and you're ready to go.

stripe		stripe		stripe
	dog		cat	
stripe				stripe
	cat		dog	
stripe		stripe		stripe

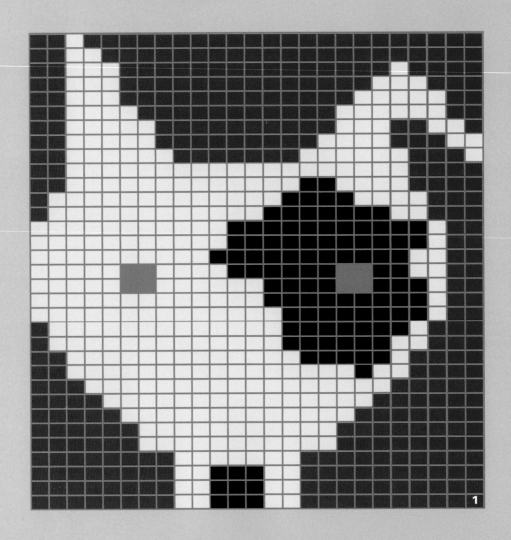

Dog Chart
25 sts x 33 rows

Wake up kitty!

Saunter down to page 81 to see another picture

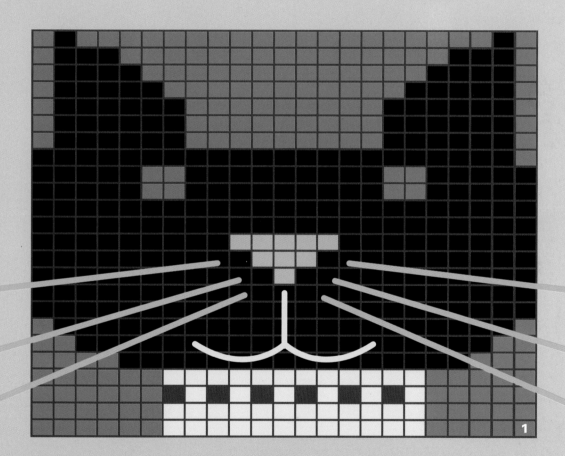

Cat Chart
23 sts x 24 rows
Use backstitch for mouth and whiskers

Playful Pooches

Bandanas

These cool bandanas are ideal for the more macho dog. Oozing with attitude, there are two great designs to choose from.

Superstar
Materials and Equipment
* Sirdar Luxury Soft Cotton DK in:
  Ruby Red, 1 x 1¾oz (50g) ball
  Vanilla Cream, 1 x 1¾oz (50g) ball
* 4mm (US 6) needles
* Brass eyelets and tool
* Red cord, 1yd (30cm)

Skull and Crossbones
Materials and Equipment
* Sirdar Bonus DK in:
  Navy, 1 x 3½oz (100g) ball
  Red, 1 x 3½oz (100g) ball
  Cream, 1 x 3½oz (100g) ball
* 4mm (US 6) needles
* Brass eyelets and tool
* Red or navy cord, 1yd (30cm)

Tension
22 sts x 30 rows per 4in (10cm)

Sizing
One size

Pattern for both Bandanas
Using 4mm (US 6) needles and **Ruby Red for Superstar** or **Navy for Skull and Crossbones** CO 2 sts.
Row 1: Inc into both sts (4 sts).
Row 2: P.
Row 3: Inc into first st, K2, inc into last st (6 sts).

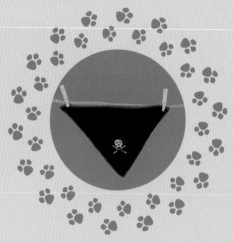

Row 4: P.
Row 5: Inc into first st, K to last st, inc into last st (8 sts).
Row 6: P.
For Skull and Crossbones: Repeat rows 5 and 6, increasing by 2 stitches on every RS row until you have 76 sts ending on a RS row.
For Superstar: Repeat rows 5 and 6, increasing by 2 stitches on every RS row until you have 26 sts ending on a WS row.
Begin intarsia chart as follows:
Next Row: Inc into first st, K3, work row 1 of the Superstar chart (see page 92), K2, inc into last st.
Continue working from the chart

as set **at the same time** still increasing by two stitches on every RS row until the chart is complete. Now, using Ruby Red as before, continue working the increases until 76 sts ending on a RS row.
If working the Skull and Crossbones pattern, change to Ruby Red.
Next 2 Rows: K.
Cast off evenly in garter st.

Sides
Using Ruby Red for Superstar and Red for Skull and Crossbones, with 4mm (US 6) needles and with RS facing, PUK 66 sts along left side.
Next Row: Cast off knitwise.
Repeat for second side.

Finishing

Weave in loose ends and **if making the Skull and Crossbone** design use Swiss darning (Duplicate stitch) and cream yarn to fix it in place. (Remember to centre the logo first by folding the bandana in half and marking the centre with a pin.) Find the centre of the chart and work outwards accordingly. After embellishing, carefully push a brass eyelet through the fabric of the right top corner and fix with the tool. Repeat in the opposite corner. Now, thread through your cord and slip over your dog's head for measurement. Finally, snip to length and tie a knot in each end to prevent it fraying.

Worked in double knit, they are quick and simple to make and tie with a cord around the neck.

I have used brass eyelets on the top corners for strength and appearance; you should find these readily available in most good haberdashers and my pack came with the eyelet tool included, so they were very simple to fix in place. However, if you prefer, you could substitute a yarn over buttonhole instead. Just remember to work one into each end of the last few rows of the pattern.

Fetch!

Go to page **80** to see more pictures

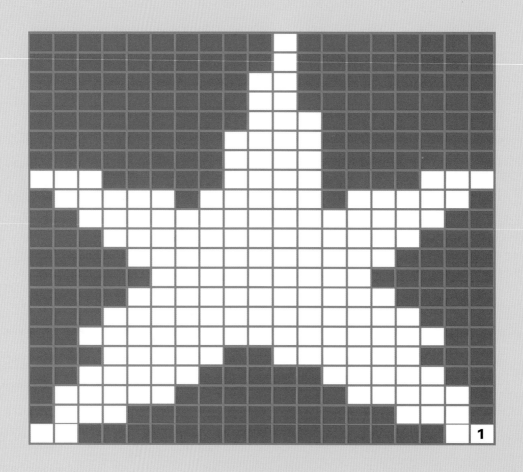

Superstar Chart
19 sts x 21 rows

Knits for dogs and cats

Skull and Crossbones Chart
9 sts x 11 rows

Fur Bone

This furry bone cushion is the height of luxury for you and your pooch.

Materials and Equipment
* Sirdar Bonus Chunky in Black, 1 x 3½oz (100g) ball
* Sirdar Foxy in Arctic Fox, 2 x 1¾oz (50g) balls
* 8mm (US 11) needles
* Washable toy stuffing

Tension
Unimportant.

Back
With Black Chunky and 8mm (US 11) needles CO 6 sts.
Row 1: Inc into first st, K to last st, inc into last s (8 sts).
Row 2: K.
Rep these two rows until 18 sts. Break thread, push work to end of needle and ignore for a moment. On the same needle, using Black Chunky, CO 6 sts and rep the above stages until 18 sts.
Now, knit across both pieces of work to join them as one (36 sts in total).
Rep rows 1 and 2 once (38 sts).
Next Row: K2tog, K to last 2 sts, K2tog.
Next Row: K.
Rep these last two decreasing rows until 30 sts on needle. Work even in garter st for 8in (20.5cm). Now rep rows 1 and 2 until 38 sts.

Next Row: K2tog, K to last 2 sts, K2tog (36 sts).
Next Row: K18 sts. Turn.
Working on these 18 sts only, decrease as follows:
Next Row: K2tog, K to last 2 sts, K2tog.
Next Row: K.
Rep these two rows until 6 sts left on needle then cast off.
Rejoin yarn to the remaining 18 sts and rep as shaping as above.

Front
Work the same as for back but using Sirdar Foxy and 8mm (US 11) needles.

Finishing
With right sides facing, sew the two pieces together, leaving a small opening and a tail of yarn along one side. Turn work right side out and fill generously with washable toy stuffing. Finally, using the tail of yarn, sew up remaining hole with small stitches.

Filled with washable toy stuffing, this cute cushion is designed to be thrown into the washing machine when it gets a bit tired and over-loved. Line his basket with it so he can slumber in maximum comfort. You could even steal it for yourself. That's if your best pal can be persuaded to part with it, of course!

Fetch!
Go to page **78** to see more pictures

Fur bone

Cable Twist Scarf

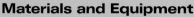

If you're new to the cable technique, then this scarf is the ideal starting place.

Materials and Equipment

- Stylecraft Aran in Moss,
  1 x 17½oz (500g) ball
- 5mm (US 8) needles
- 1 wooden button

Tension

18 sts and 24 rows to 4in (10cm)

Sizing

To fit 9[12:14:17]in
(23[30.5:35.5:43.5]cm) neck

Special Abbreviations

4 sts cbbk: Sl 2 sts to cn
and hold to back of work, K2,
K2 from cn
4 sts cbfr: Sl 2 sts to cn
and hold in front of work, K2,
K2 from cn

Pattern

With Stylecraft Aran and 5mm
(US 8) needles CO 20 sts.
Begin cable pattern as follows:
Row 1: K1, P1, K1, P1, P2, K8, P2,
P1, K1, P1, K1.
Row 2: K1, P1, K1, P1, K2, P8, K2,
P1, K1, P1, K1.
Rep. rows 1 and 2 once more.
Row 5: K1, P1, K1, P1, P2, 4 sts
cbbk, 4 sts cbfr, P2, P1, K1, P1, K1.
Row 6: As row 2.
These six rows form the pattern.
Keep repeating them until work
measures approx. 14[18:21:25]in

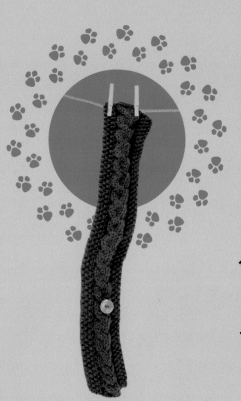

(35.5[46:53.5:63.5]cm) ending on
row 2.
Now work the buttonhole as
follows:
Next Row: K1, P1, K1, P1, P2, K4,
yf, K2 tog, K2, P2, P1, K1, P1, K1.
Continue in patt as set until work
measures 19[24:28:33]in
(48.5[61:71:84]cm) ending
on a WS row then cast off.

Finishing

Weave in any loose ends then sew
on a wooden button. Measuring up
from the opposite end of the
buttonhole end, attach the button
5[6:7:8]in (12.5[15:18:20.5]cm)
from the bottom.

Once you've got the basic pattern mastered, it's easy-going all the way to the end with no difficult shaping to trip you up. Instead of a thread-through, I've added a button to keep the scarf snugly in place. It's an Aran knit, too, so it'll grow fast enough to keep you interested.

Fetch! Go to page **81** to see another picture

Doggy Bag

Materials and Equipment

- Stylecraft Icicle in Crystal, 2 x 1¾oz (50g) balls
- Sirdar Chunky in Black, 1 x 3¾oz (100g) balls
- 3 sheets of plastic canvas, 14 x 22in (35.5 x 56cm)
- Parcel string for sewing body
- Pink and black cotton thread
- Small- and large-eyed sewing needles
- Black webbing, 1in (2.5cm)
- Pink quilted lining, 3⅓ft (1m)
- Piece of heavy-duty card (i.e. picture framing board), 7½ x 14in (19 x 35.5cm)
- Small piece of black mesh plus bias binding for front pocket
- 8mm (US 11) needles

Sizing

Suitable for small dogs only – weight up to 7lbs (3kg).

Always check straps are secure before transporting your pet.

Bag Body

Follow the diagram on page 100 to cut the plastic canvas body of your bag to size. Use parcel string and a large-eyed needle to sew it all together (see sewing guide for canvas at the top of page 100); the holes in the canvas make this easier than you might think.

Now pop your heavy-duty card into the bottom of the bag for reinforcement.

Lining

Use the Lining diagram on page 101 to cut your pink quilted material to size. Remember to allow at least ½in (1.5cm) extra for seams and overlap. With RS facing, pin and sew the rear side seams of the lining so that you have a 3D shape which echoes the plastic bag body. Drop your lining inside the body, fold the seam allowance of the lining down around the top edge of the bag then pin in place.

Now, using a small-eyed needle and pink thread, sew firmly around all edges so the lining is completely fastened to the plastic body of the bag. Don't worry too much about neatness, as this stitching will subsequently be covered up by the bag's outer layer. I put a few extra stitches at the base of the bag, just at the corner points, to anchor the lining more firmly at the bottom.

Front Pocket

Cut your black mesh according to the Pocket diagram on page 101 then fold a length of black bias binding along the top edge to enclose the raw edge. Stitch firmly in place. Now pin the pocket across the front opening of the bag, taking care to retain the rectangular box shape of the carrier. Pin in place along the side and bottom and then stitch to secure.

Outer Layer
Bottom

Using 8mm (US 11) needles and Black Chunky CO 24 sts. Beginning with a K row, work in st st for 14in (35.5cm) then cast off. Now turn the tote bag upside-down. With RS facing towards you, pin in place and secure with a firm stitch.

You've traipsed the town for all those sale bargains and even your stilettoed feet are burning. What hope has your poor pooch got, trying to keep up?

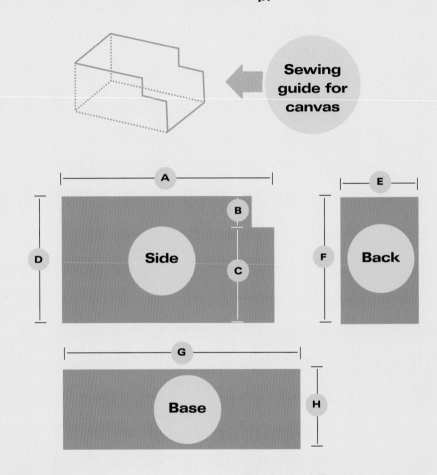

Sewing guide for canvas

Main Outer Layer

Using Icicle and 8mm (US 11) needles CO 28 sts. Garter st for 1½in (4cm). CO 12 sts at the beg of next row and garter st straight for 34in (86.5cm) ending on a WS row. Cast off 12 sts at beg of next row and garter st for 1½in (4cm). Cast off. Place outer layer around the bag then pin, making sure the under layers are covered and the top and bottom edges meet neatly. Using pink thread, stitch firmly into position.

Straps – Make 2

Using 8mm (US 11) needles and Black Chunky CO 11 sts. Beginning with a K row, st st for 50in (127cm) then cast off. With RS facing, fold strap in half lengthways and stitch along seam. Turn RS out and thread the black webbing through the centre to reinforce. Take some black thread and put a running stitch through the three layers along the length of both straps to prevent the webbing from twisting inside the knitted outer layer. Attach very firmly to your bag according to the diagram at the bottom of page 101.

Side *(cut 2)*

- **A** 14in (35.5cm)
- **B** 3in (8cm)
- **C** 7in (18cm)
- **D** 10in (25.5cm)

Back and Base *(cut 1 of each)*

- **E** 10in (25.5cm)
- **F** 7½in (19cm)
- **G** 14in (35.5cm)
- **H** 7½in (19cm)

The Doggy Bag is ideal for times like these, when your doggy's drooping or your puppy's plain pooped. I've used over-the-top pink fun fur for the ultimate in celebrity-style glamour but the plastic canvas body makes a substantial and practical carrier for your best pal.

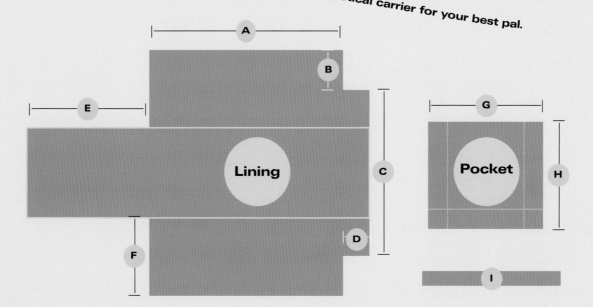

Lining *(add ¾in (19mm) in seam allowance on every edge)*

A 14in (35.6cm)

B 3in (8cm)

C 22in (56cm)

D 1 ½in (4cm)

E 10in (25.5cm)

F 10in (25.5cm)

Pocket *(with allowances)*

G 8in (20cm)

H 9in (23cm)

I Bias binding strip

Fetch! Go to page **81** to see another picture

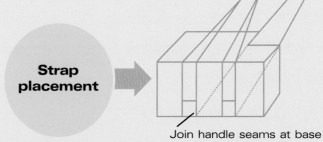

Strap placement

Join handle seams at base

Shoe Chew

This stylish stiletto is the perfect toy for your puppy and it might just save your more expensive Jimmy Choos if your puppy likes to chew.

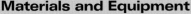

Materials and Equipment

❧ Patons 100% Cotton DK in:
Foxglove, shade 02706,
1 x 3½oz (100g) ball
Nougat, shade 02715,
1 x 3½oz (100g) ball
Black, shade 02712,
1 x 3½oz (100g) ball
❧ Small length of burgundy ribbon
❧ Washable polyester toy stuffing
❧ 1 small bell
❧ 3.25mm (US 3) needles.
❧ Stitch marker
❧ Stitch holder

Upper

Using Foxglove and 3.25mm (US 3) needles CO 3 sts and work 2 rows in st st.
Row 1: Inc into first st, K and PM on this centre st, inc into last st.
Row 2: P.
Row 3: K to st before centre st, inc into next st, K centre st, inc into next st, K to end (7 st).
Row 4: P.
Rep rows 3 and 4, always inc one st either side of centre st. until you have 33 sts, ending on a WS row. Still working in st st, cast off 4 sts at beg of next 2 rows (25 sts).
Next Row: K2tog, K7, inc into last st (10 sts). Turn and leave rem sts on a stitch holder.

Working on these 10 sts only, P the next row.
Row 1: K2tog, K7, inc into last st (10 sts).
Row 2: P.
Rep rows 1 and 2 for 2in (5cm) ending on a row 2.
Next Row: Inc into first st, K to end.
Next Row: P.
Rep. the last two rows once more (12 sts).
Work in st st for 2in (5cm). Cast off. Rejoin thread to front of shoe. Cast off the first 5 sts and K to end. (10 sts). P the next row.
Row 1: Inc into first st, K to last 2 sts, K2tog. (10 sts).
Row 2: P.

Rep these 2 rows for 2in (5cm).
Next Row: K to last st, inc into last st.
Next Row: P.
Rep these 2 rows once more (12 sts).
Work in st st for 2in (5cm). Cast off. Fold shoe upper in half lengthways with RS facing and then sew rear seam together.

Sole

Using Black and 3.25mm (US 3) needles CO 3 sts. St st 2 rows.
Row 1: Inc into first st, K to end, inc into last st (5 sts).
Row 2: P.
Rows 3: K.
Row 4: P.
Rep these 4 rows until 21 sts ending on row 2.
Next Row: K2tog, K to last 2 sts, K2tog.
Next Row: P.
Rep these last 2 rows until 9 sts. Work in st st for 1½in (4cm) ending on a WS row.
Next Row: Inc into first st, K to last st, inc into last st (11 sts).
Next Row: P.
Rep once more (13 sts).
Work even in st st for 6 rows.
Next Row: K2tog, K to last 2 sts, K2tog.
Next Row: P2tog, P to last 2 sts, P2tog.

Fetch!

Go to page **79** to see another picture

Rep these two rows until 5 sts left. Cast off and tidy loose ends.

Top

With RS facing, and using Nougat and 3.25mm (US 3) needles, PUK 5 sts across centre front cast-off edge and work 2 rows in st st.

Row 1: Inc into first st, K to last st, inc into last st (7 sts).

Row 2: P.

Row 3: K.

Row 4: P.

Rep these last 4 rows until 15 sts ending on a row 2.

Work 2 rows in st st.

Next Row: K2tog, K to last 2 sts, K2tog (13 sts).

Next Row: P2tog, P to last 2 sts, P2tog (11 sts).

Rep these two rows until 5 sts left.

Next Row: P.

Cast off and tidy loose ends.

Heel

Using Black and 3.25mm (US 3) needles CO 20 sts and st st for 2 rows.

Next Row: *K2, K2tog* rep from * to * to end of row (15 sts).

Next Row: P.

Rep these last two rows once more (12 sts).

Next Row: *K2tog * rep from * to * to end of row (6 sts).

Work in st st for 1in (2.5cm) ending on a WS row.

Next Row: K2tog three times (3 sts) Break yarn leaving a long tail, thread through sts and pull tight.

Making Up

With RS edges facing, pin the pink top to the shoe upper and sew in place with small backstitches. With RS facing, place the upper to the sole, pin in place and sew together with small backstitches. Make sure to leave a 1in (2.5cm) opening for turning and stuffing. Turn the shoe right side out and fill firmly with the polyester toy stuffing. Pop the bell into the toe area, wedging it firmly with stuffing. Once the upper is plump and full, sew up the opening with small stitches. Now take the heel and with RS facing, sew up the rear seam. Turn the heel right side out and pack the spike with toy

stuffing. This can be a little fiddly as the heel is very narrow. If you get into difficulty, use the head of your knitting needle to coax the stuffing to the bottom. Now place the heel top to the underside of the shoe. Sew firmly in place with small stitches. You can embellish your stiletto upper with a bow or embroidery if you're feeling flamboyant but remember to sew the ribbon on firmly so it can't be chewed off.

It comes with a jingly bell inside the toe, so you'll always know exactly where he is, too.

Common sense is the order of the day with puppies and knitted toys. Sew all seams firmly and if yours is a chewer, in order to avoid large vet bills, keep a close eye for torn seams and loose bells or stuffing.

Shoe chew

Pampered Kitties

Fish Cushion

This fish cushion is so simple to make, and your cat will love it.

Materials and Equipment
- Sirdar Luxury Soft Cotton DK in:
  Ruby Red,
  1 x 1¾oz (50g) ball
  Vanilla Cream,
  1 x 1¾oz (50g) ball
  Lamp Black,
  1 x 1¾oz (50g) ball
- 4mm (US 6) needles
- Small piece of white felt
- Washable polyester toy stuffing
- Sewing needle and white
  cotton thread

Tension
22 sts x 28 rows over
4in (10cm)

Sizing
Finished cushion is 12in (30.5cm)
in diameter

Fish Body – Make 2
Using 4mm (US 6) needles and
Red CO 14 sts. Starting with a
K row, beg working in st st.
Inc 1 st into first and last st of
every row until 66 sts.
When you have completed the
increases, work even until patt
states otherwise.
At the same time, work stripe
sequence as follows:
3in (8cm) in Red, ending on a
WS row

4 rows Black
1½in (4cm) in Cream ending on a
WS row
4 rows Black
1½in (4cm) in Red ending on WS
row
2 rows Black.
Now begin decreases as follows:
K2tog at beginning and end of
next and every following row until
14 sts rem ending on a WS row.

At the same time, continue in stripe
sequence as follows:
2 rows Black
1½in (4cm) Cream ending on a
WS row
2 rows Black
1½in (4cm) (or until you reach 14
st) in Red ending on a WS row.
Cast off

Dorsal Fins – Make 2
Using 4mm (US 6) needles and
Black CO 2 sts. Starting with a K
row begin working in st st, inc 1
st into first and last st of next and
every following row until 52 sts
ending on a WS row.
Work 2 rows even in st st.
Cast off.
Finishing: With RS together, fold
the fin in half lengthways and sew
the side seam. Turn right side out
and then fill firmly with polyester
toy stuffing.

Rear Fin – Make 2
Using 4mm (US 6) needles and
Black CO 14 sts.
Beg with a K row, work 4 rows in
st st.
Next Row: Inc into first and last st
of this and every alt row until 36
sts ending on a P row.
Work 2 rows even in st st.
Cast off.

Finishing: With RS together, pin and sew side seams together. Follow the stitching diagram on the right to sew the top seam (the widest part). This will form the double fin. Turn right side out and stuff firmly.

Final Finishing

With RS facing upwards, lay one body piece on a flat surface. Pin and stitch the fins in place as shown right. Now place the second body piece on top like a giant sandwich with RS facing inwards and pin and sew the whole fish together leaving a 1in (2.5cm) opening for stuffing. Turn your fish right side out and stuff firmly. Sew up the opening with small neat stitches. Next, use the eye template to cut out two pieces of white felt. Use a length of black yarn to embroider the black pupil. Pin the eye in place and sew with small, neat stitches.

Rear Fin Stitching Diagram

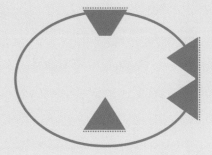

Fish Sewing Guide

Key

Stitching line

Eye Template
Reproduce at 100%

Template

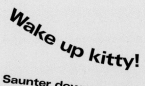
Wake up kitty!
Saunter down to page 80 to see another picture

Fish cushion

Princess Pussycat
Throne

Materials and Equipment

- Sirdar Wow in Imperial Purple, shade 760, 3 x 3½oz (100g) balls
- Sirdar Bonus Chunky in Violet, shade 985, 1 x 3½oz (100g) ball
- Patons Whisper in Crystal, shade 00008, 2 x 1¾oz (50g) balls
- Patons Spritz in Spritzer, shade 03001, 1 x 1¾oz (50g) balls
- 3 glass beads
- 1in (2.5cm) wide black Velcro tape, 10in (25.5cm)
- 6mm (US 10), 4mm (US 6), 8mm (US 11) needles
- Washable polyester toy stuffing

Tension

Base: 14 sts x 19 rows to 4in (10cm) using Sirdar Bonus Chunky and 6mm (US 10) needles
Top: 22 sts x 30 rows to 4in (10cm) using Patons Whisper and 4mm (US 6) needles.
Sides: 8 sts x 15 rows to 4in (10cm) using Sirdar Wow and 7mm (US 11) needles.

Base

Using Sirdar Chunky and 6mm (US 10) needles CO 10 st and st st for 2 rows.
Continuing in st st, inc 1 st at each

end of next and every row until 50 sts. Work until work measures 10½in (26.5cm).
Dec 1 st at each end of next and every row until 22 sts.
Cast off.

Top

Using Patons Whisper and 4mm (US 6) needles CO 16 sts.
Working in st st, inc 1 st at each end of next and every row until 76 sts.
Work until work measures 10½in (27cm).
Dec 1 st at each end of next and every row until 34 sts. Cast off.

Sides

Using Sirdar Wow and 8mm (US 11) needles CO 5 sts.
Work even in st st for 42in (107cm). Cast off.

Finishing Base

With RS together, pin and sew the sidepiece together at its shortest edge. You now have a long, circular strip. Pin this onto the base with RS together. Make sure the side seam is at the centre of the base's cast-off seam. Sew in place.
Now, with RS together, pin the top piece and sew in place, leaving a small opening for stuffing. Turn RS out and stuff the bottom cushion quite firmly, although your cat might like a little dip in the centre to nestle into. Sew up the opening.

Throne Back – Make 2

Using Sirdar Wow and 8mm (US 11) needles CO 16 sts.
Working in st st, work 11in (28cm).
Next Row: Ssk, K to last 2 st, K2tog.
Next Row: P.
Rep these two rows until 1st.
Fasten off.

Throne Sides

Using Sirdar Wow and 8mm (US 11) needles CO 4 sts. Work in st st for 40in (102cm). Cast off.

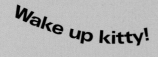 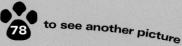
Crown

Using Patons Spritz and 4mm
(US 6) needles CO 15 sts.
Rows 1–3: K.
Row 4: P.
Row 5: K.
Row 6: P.
Rows 7–9: K.
Row 10: P.
Work even in st st until crown
measures 3in (8cm) ending with
a P row.
Divide for prongs as follows:
K5 sts. Turn.
Working on these 5 sts work even
in st st for 2in (5cm) ending on a
P row.
Next Row: K2tog, K1, K2tog (3 sts).
Next Row: P3tog. Fasten off.
Returning to the rest of the stitches
on your needle, rep the above
twice more.

Finishing Throne Back

Take the throne sides and with RS
tog, sew the short ends together
to give you a long, narrow circular
strip. Next take the first throne back
and with RS tog, pin the sidepiece
around the edge of the throne
back. Make sure the side seam is
positioned at the bottom of the
throne back. Sew in place. Now,
take the second throne back and
with RS together, pin and sew to

the other side edge, leaving a small
opening for stuffing. Turn RS out, fill
the throne back firmly with toy
stuffing then sew up the opening.
Pin the crown to the front of
throne back and sew in place with
small stitches. Take your glass
beads and sew one at each point
of the crown.

Final Finishing

Lastly, you'll need to attach the
base cushion to the throne back,
so stand your throne up and pin
the Velcro in place. You'll need one
strip along the rear edge of the
base and the other on the bottom
edge of the throne back. Tack and
sew firmly in place before offering
the finished throne to your beloved
moggy for a yawn of approval.

My mother's cat, Jet, moved into her house, a scraggy old stray with only one front tooth and a very bad temper. But to Mum, Jet was King of the household and far more beautiful than the most expensive pedigree Persian.

When her husband finally lost his favourite armchair to the manipulative little moggy, we used to joke that Mum would be installing a throne for the little furball next! With a regal yawn and a wink, Jet almost seemed to agree. So for pampered pusscats everywhere, here it is, the Princess Pussycat Throne – a cat-bed fit for the King (or Queen) of your household.

Position Velcro at base of throne back and rear edge of base cushion

Kitten Mittens

All kittens love to play, and this Kitten Mitten is the ideal toy for pet and owner bonding sessions.

Moody Blue
Materials and Equipment
- Elle Mexican Wave DK in Moody Blue, 1 x 3$\frac{1}{2}$oz (100g) ball
- Sirdar Bonus DK in:
  Navy Blue,
  1 x 3$\frac{1}{2}$oz (100g) ball
  Signal Red,
  1 x 3$\frac{1}{2}$oz (100g) ball
- 4mm (US 6) needles
- 2 brass bells
- 1 small recycled denim pocket (the more beaten up the better)
- Catnip or toy stuffing

Dear Heart
Materials and Equipment
- Rowan Handknit Cotton in:
  Slick, shade 313,
  1 x 1$\frac{3}{4}$oz (50g) ball
  Gooseberry, shade 219,
  1 x 1$\frac{3}{4}$oz (50g) ball
  Yellow Zing, shade 300,
  1 x 1$\frac{3}{4}$oz (50g) ball
- 3.25mm (US 3), 3.5mm (US 4) and 4mm (US 6) needles
- 2 brass bells
- 7 gold sequins
- Polyester toy stuffing

Sizing
One size fits all

Tension for Moody Blue
22 sts x 30 rows to 4in (10cm) using DK and 4mm (US 6) needles

Tension for Dear Heart
20 sts x 28 rows using 4mm (US 6) needles

Moody Blue Pattern
Using Navy Blue and 4mm (US 6) needles CO 48 sts.
Change to your main colour – Elle Mexican Wave – and beg cuff as follows:
Row 1: P2, *K4, P4 * rep from * to * to last 2 sts- P2.

Row 2: K2, *P4, K4 * rep from * to * to last 2 sts- K2.
Rows 3–4: as rows 1 and 2.
Row 5: P2, *C4f, P4 * rep from * to * to last 2 st- P2.
Row 6: As row 2.
Rep rows 1–6 until cuff measures 2in (5cm).
Next Row : K2tog, K to last 2 sts, K2tog (46 sts).
Next Row: P.
Rep the last two rows once more (44 sts).

**Thumb Gusset
Next Row: K25, (K1, P1, K1) into next st, K to end (46 sts).
Work 5 rows in st st.
Next Row: K25, * (K1, P1, K1) into next st * K1, rep from * to * once more, K to end (50 sts).
Work 5 rows in st st.
Next Row: K25, * (K1, P1, K1) into next st * K5 rep from * to * once more, K to end (54 sts).
Work 5 rows in st st.
Next Row: K25 * (K1, P1, K1) into next st * K9 rep from * to * once more, K to end (58 sts in total).

Divide for Thumb
P35. Turn.
Next Row: CO 2 st, K18, turn.
Work 15 rows in st st on these 18 sts ending on a P row.

Shape Top

Next Row: Still working in st st, K2tog at each end of next 7 rows (4 sts).

Next Row: P2tog twice.

Break yarn and thread thru rem sts. Pull tight then sew up thumb seam. With RS side facing, rejoin yarn at base of thumb.

First Finger

PUK 3 sts at base of thumb and K across row until end.

Next Row: P (45 sts in total).

Work 15 rows (**13 rows if working Dear Heart version**) in st st ending on a K row.

Next row: P29, turn.

Next Row: CO2 sts, K15, turn

Work 19 rows on these 15 sts.

Shape Top

K2tog at each end of row for 6 rows (3 sts).

Next Row: K3tog.

Break yarn, thread thru rem sts and pull tight. Sew up finger seam. With RS facing, rejoin yarn at base of first finger.

Second Finger

PUK 3 sts at base of first finger, K6, turn.

Next Row: CO2 sts, P17, turn.

Work 22 rows on these 17 sts.

Shape Top

K2tog at each end of next 7 rows (3 sts).

Next Row: K3tog.

Break yarn, thread thru rem st and pull tight. Sew finger seam. With RS facing, rejoin yarn at base of second finger

Third Finger

PUK 3 sts across base of second finger, K5, turn.

Next Row: CO2 st, P16, turn.

Work 18 rows on these 16 sts.

Shape Top

K2tog at each end of next 8 rows (1 st).

Break yarn, thread thru rem st and pull tight. Sew finger seam. With RS facing, rejoin yarn at base of third finger.

Fourth Finger

PUK3 sts across base of third finger, K5, turn.

Next Row: P12.

Work 14 rows on these 12 sts.

Shape Top

K2tog at each end of next 6 rows. (1 st).

Break yarn, thread thru rem st and pull tight. Sew up finger seam. **

Fishing Line and Catnip Fish

Using Navy and Red yarn, make a twisted cord approx 16in (41cm) long. Of course, you can adjust the length according to preference.

Fish – Make 2

Using Navy yarn and 4mm (US 6) needles CO 10 sts.

Working in st st, dec 1 st at each end of next and every alt row until 2 sts ending on a P row.

Change to Red.

Row 1: Inc, 1 st at each end of this K row (4 sts).

Row 2: P.

Change to Navy.

Keeping to stripe patt, rep rows 1 and 2, until 8 sts.

St st next 2 rows and change to Navy.

Dec 1 st at each end of next and every alt row until 2 sts.

Break yarn, thread through rem sts and pull tight.

Sew the two pieces tog leaving a small opening for stuffing.

Thread the cord thru the fish's nose and secure.

Now fill firmly with catnip or toy stuffing and sew up the opening.

Choose the denim version for tough boys or the cuter heart mitten for your little girl.

Finishing

Darn in loose ends and sew up the side seam of the glove. Pin and sew the denim pocket in place then sew brass bells firmly to the tip of the first and third finger. Make two, 3in (8cm) navy blue and red tassels and attach them to the thumb and fourth fingertip. Finally, make the fishing line and catnip fish as detailed and attach to middle finger. Now go find your kitty and enjoy!

Dear Heart Pattern

Cuff

Using Gooseberry and 3.25mm (US 3) needles CO 44 sts.
Change to Slick.
Row 1: *K1, P1 * rep from * to * to end.
Row 2: As row 1.
Change to Yellow Zing
Rows 3–4: As row 1.
Change to Gooseberry
Rows 5–6: As row 1.
Change to Slick.
Rep this stripe sequence until cuff measures 2in (5cm) ending on row 2.
Change to 3.5mm (US 3) needles and Slick.
Beg with a K row, work in st st for 4 rows. Now proceed as for the Moody Blue glove from ** to **.

Pocket

Now work the pocket using the chart on page 119 and 3.5mm (US 3) needles. Sew a few sequins in place to give the heart motif a bit of sparkle. Tidy the ends, pin onto front of the glove and sew neatly in place.

Heart and Line

First make the line by plaiting three lengths of Slick to make a 16in (41cm) cord. Knot each end.

Stuffed Heart – Make 2

Using Slick and 3.25mm (US 3) needles CO 2 sts.
Beg with a K row work stripe sequence in st st as follows.
Rows 1–2: Slick.
Rows 3–4: Gooseberry.
Rows 5–6: Yellow Zing.
At the same time, inc 1 st into first and last st of every row until 14 sts.
Work stripe sequence as set for a further 6 rows.
Keeping to stripe patt divide for top of heart as follows:
Next Row: K2tog, K5 turn (6 sts).
Work on these 6 sts only.
Next Row: P2tog, P4, turn (5 sts).
Next Row: K2tog, K3, turn (4 sts).
Next Row: P2tog, P2, turn (3 sts).
Work 2 rows even on these 3 sts.

Cast off.
Rejoin yarn to the rem 7 sts.
Keeping to stripe patt, work as for first side, reversing shapings.
Cast off.

Finishing

Tidy yarn ends and with RS facing, sew together leaving a small opening for stuffing. Turn right side out and thread your plaited cord through the top of the heart. Now stuff firmly and sew up the opening neatly.

Final Finishing

Sew brass bells firmly to the first and third fingertips. Attach the heart and line to the middle finger of the glove. Using Gooseberry and Yellow Zing, make a 3in (8cm) tassel and sew firmly to the thumb. Using all three colours, make a 2in (5cm) pompom and attach to the fourth finger.

Wake up kitty!

Saunter down to page 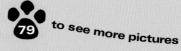 79 to see more pictures

As with all pet toys, sew bells, tassels, and so on very firmly. To ensure Kitty's good health, always keep a close eye on any loose components, making sure to re-stitch and replace when necessary.

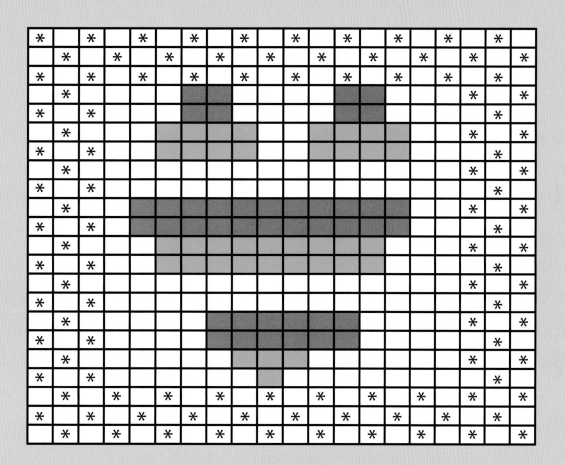

Heart Chart

Each square = 1 st and 1 row

Read RS rows from R to L and WS rows from L to R

Moss stitch in slick as are all white squares

The Basics

Knitting Know-how

Knitting Essentials

Yarns

It is a good idea to buy the yarns specified in my patterns, of which there are a range to suit every budget, so that you are sure the finished garment will look as good as the picture. If you are not sure where to buy a yarn, contact the supplier for stockists' details (see page 137). Also, remember that yarn is dyed in batches or lots, so check the dye lot on the label. Make sure the numbers match, otherwise there may be some colour variation when you change balls.

If you want to substitute the yarns in a pattern there are several points to bear in mind. Always substitute for the same weight of yarn (for US yarn conversions see page 139). Always check the yardage on the label of your preferred yarn – this may vary from the amount on the recommended type, and the amount you require may need some careful working out. Also, before you start, knit up a tension swatch in your substitute yarn to check that the stitch sizes match so that the finished garment is the correct size and to give you a better idea of how it will look.

Tension Swatches

To knit a tension swatch, cast on 40 stitches using the recommended needle size. Work in the pattern for a minimum of 4in (10cm) before casting off loosely. Next, lay the swatch out on a flat surface and place a ruler vertically on top. Count the number of rows over 4in (10cm). Then do the same horizontally, but this time count the number of stitches over 4in (10cm). If you have more stitches and rows than stated on the pattern, try knitting the swatch again with larger needles. Likewise, if there are fewer stitches and rows, repeat with smaller needles. Keep working until your tension matches that of the pattern.

Following Instructions

Before you begin knitting, always read the pattern from start to finish. It's a good idea to underline the size you are knitting throughout the pattern so you know exactly where you are at a glance. Figures for larger sizes are given in square brackets. Where only one figure appears, this applies to all sizes. Finally, check any abbreviations you are not sure of on page 138 and, just like following a recipe, gather all your yarn, tools, buttons and trimmings before you start.

Reading Charts

Some of my patterns use cable and colour charts. As in all knitting charts, one square represents one stitch and one line of squares is equal to one row.

On right-side rows, read the chart from right to left, and on wrong-side rows read from left to right. Start from the bottom right-side corner of the chart at row 1. Carry on to rows 2 and 3, and so on, until the chart is complete.

You will see that every square has either a symbol or a colour marked on it. Read the accompanying key to understand which colour or stitch you will need to use to complete the row.

A chart ruler (available from most good haberdashers or yarn stores) is an excellent investment. You can clip it onto the chart and move it up or down the rows once completed. That way you won't get muddled or lost in the middle.

Some charts, such as Fair Isle or Cable, have 'repeats' included in them. In this case, complete the whole chart to the end and then start over again at row 1.

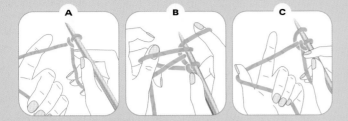

Basic Stitches

Casting On (see above)

1. Make a slipknot a fair distance from the end of the yarn and place it onto your needle. Pull the knot tight to make your first stitch. **A**

2. Hold the needle in your right hand and wrap the loose tail end around your left thumb from front to back. **B**

3. Push the point of the needle through the thumb loop from front to back. **B**

4. Wind the ball end of the yarn around the needle from left to right. **B**

5. Pull the loop through the thumb loop and remove your thumb. Gently pull the new loop tight using the tail yarn. **C**

6. Repeat until you have the desired number of stitches on the needle.

Garter Stitch
Knit every row.

Stocking Stitch
Knit on right-side rows and purl on wrong-side rows.

Moss Stitch
Worked over an 'even' number of stitches as follows:

Row 1: (K1, P1) to end.
Row 2: (P1, K1) to end.
Rep rows 1 and 2 to form patt.

Worked over an 'odd' number of stitches as follows:
Row 1: *K1, P1, rep from * to last st, K1.
Rep row 1 to form patt.

Single Rib
Worked over an 'even' number of stitches as follows:

Row 1: *K1, P1* rep to end.
Rep row 1 to form patt.

Worked over an 'odd' number of stitches as follows:
Row 1: *K1, P1, rep from * to last st, K1.
Row 2: *P1, K1, rep from * to last st, P1.

Double Rib
Row 1: *K2, P2, rep from * to end.
Rep row 1 to form patt.

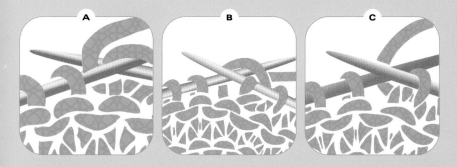

Knit Stitch (see above)

1. Hold the needle with the stitches in your left hand. Hold the yarn at back of the work and insert the point of the right-hand empty needle into the front loop of the first stitch. **A**

2. Wrap the yarn around the point of the right-hand needle in a clockwise direction using your index finger. Bring the yarn through to the front of the work. **A**

3. With the yarn still wrapped around the point, bring the right-hand needle back towards you through the loop of the first stitch. Try to keep the free yarn fairly taut but not too slack or tight. **B**

4. Finally, with the new stitch firmly on the right-hand needle, gently pull the old stitch to the right and off the tip of the left-hand needle. **C**

5. Repeat for all the knit stitches across the row.

Purl Stitch (see below)

1. Hold the needle with the stitches in your left hand. Hold the yarn at front of the work and insert the point of right-hand empty needle into the front loop of the first stitch. **A**

2. Wrap the yarn around the point of the right-hand needle in an anticlockwise direction using your index finger. Bring the yarn back to the front of the work. **B**

3. Now with the yarn still wrapped around the point of the right-hand needle, bring it back through the stitch. Try to keep the free yarn taut but not too slack or tight. **C**

4. Finally, with the new stitch firmly on the right-hand needle, gently pull the old stitch off the tip of the left-hand needle.

5. Repeat for all the purl stitches along the row.

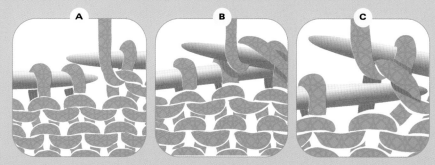

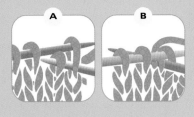

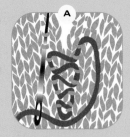

For invisible seams when making up using Mattress Stitch, join pieces together with matching yarn.

Casting Off (see above left and centre)

1. Knit the first two stitches.

2. Push the point of the left needle through the first stitch and lift over the second stitch. One stitch remains on the right needle. **A**

3. Knit another stitch from the left needle and repeat steps 2 and 3. **B**

4. Repeat until you have one stitch left. Cut the yarn, leaving a long tail, and thread it through the remaining stitch and pull it tight.

Mattress Stitch (see above right)

1. Place the pieces to be joined side by side on a flat surface with the right side facing towards you.

2. Take a threaded needle and secure it to the fabric by weaving down the side edge of one of the pieces. Bring the needle out between the first and second stitches.

3. Working vertically, bring the needle back up through the opposite piece and insert into the first row again from front to back, bringing it up below the horizontal strand. **A**

4. Go back to the first piece and keep stitching in this way. You will see your stitches form a ladder along the seam. Pull tight every few stitches to close the fabric neatly.

Cable

Cables are a decorative form of twisted stitches which look really difficult but, with the help of a small accessory called a Cable Needle are surprisingly easy to do. This tiny tool enables you to knit your stitches in a different order from how they appear on the needle. The idea is that you slip a few stitches onto this needle and then come back and knit them later. Sounds hard, but try it and I assure you, you'll be impressed by the results.

The cable pattern will usually have about six or eight rows to it in total. Mostly they are knit or purl rows but it's the rows in the middle of the pattern – the ones which use the abbreviation cbbk or cbfr – which bring in the magic bit with the cable needle.

Cable 4 sts front (4 sts cbfr)

1. Slip the next 2 sts onto a cable needle and hold in front of work. **A**

2. Knit the next 2 sts from the left-hand needle as normal. Then, knit the 2 sts from the cable needle. **B**

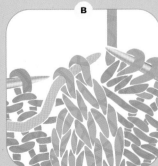

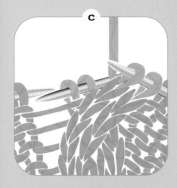

Cable 4 sts back (4 sts cbbk)

1. Slip the next 2 sts onto a cable needle and hold at back of work. **C**

2. Knit the next 2 sts from the left-hand needle as normal. Then, knit the 2 sts from the cable needle.

Variations: Where you see the instruction 6 sts cbfr or 6 sts cbbk, slip three stitches onto the cable needle and knit three stitches from the left-hand needle.

Circular Knitting

Working on Circular Needles

With the right side of the work facing you, pick up the required number of stitches onto the needle ends. Spread them out along the plastic wire. If the stitches are stretched, either use double-pointed needles or a shorter circular needle.

Place a marker onto the first stitch, so you know where the round starts and ends.

Bring the needles together and knit the first stitch, pulling the yarn tight to prevent a gap. Keep knitting, sliding the work along the wire as you go until you reach the marker. One round is now complete.

Working with Double-pointed Needles

Another method of circular knitting is to use double-pointed needles. These are particularly useful for working small numbers of stitches, such as leg holes for dog sweaters. Use a set of four, or even five for larger numbers of stitches. Remember, one needle – the working needle – always remains empty, so in the case of four needles, divide the number of stitches to be picked up or cast on by three. The stitch numbers would be divided by four if using five needles.

1. Using 4 dpns, divide the number of stitches to be picked up by three. If there are 60 stitches in total then you will have 20 stitches on each needle. **A**

2. With the right side of the work facing you, pick up 20 stitches on each needle and arrange the needles into a triangular shape. **B**

3. Place a marker on the first stitch, so you know where the round starts and ends, then knit across the first 20 stitches using the empty/working needle, making sure to pull the first stitch tight to prevent gaps.

4. Now the needle originally holding the first 20 stitches will be empty. Use this needle to knit across the second 20 stitches.

5. Now the second needle will be empty. Use this needle to knit across the third 20 stitches and to the marker. One round is complete.

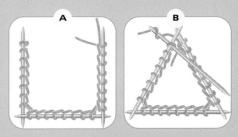

Colour Knitting

Intarsia

This technique is used when knitting blocks of colour. You will need to use separate bobbins of yarn for each isolated area of colour, as using whole balls can result in messy tangles. Bobbins are smaller and hang at the back of the work out of the way. When you need to change colours mid row, make sure you twist the old and new yarns together at the back of your work to join the blocks of colour properly and to avoid holes.

Don't worry if your work doesn't look perfect. When you have finished the piece, weave in the ends carefully at the back with a tapestry needle and press lightly under a damp cloth, easing any distorted stitches back into line. You will find this makes all the difference and can transform the neatness of your colour knitting.

Fair Isle

When knitting Fair Isle, use the stranding method, picking the colours up and dropping them as they are needed. By doing this, all the colours – including the unused ones – are carried right across the row. The loops formed by carrying are called 'floats' and should never span more than five stitches. The nature of Fair Isle knitting means you will never be working with more than two different colours across any one row.

1. Begin knitting with the first colour then drop and change to a second colour when required. When you need the first colour again, bring under the second colour and knit again. **A**

2. When you need the second colour, drop the first and bring the second colour over the first colour and knit again. **B**

3. Keep using this stranding technique at the back of the work, ensuring your floats are of even tension: not too tight, as the fabric will pucker, or too loose. Stop from time to time to ease the whole piece out.

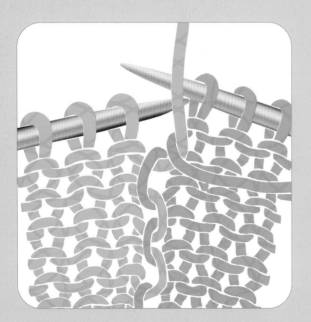

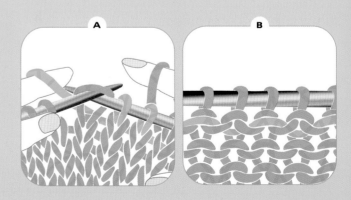

Beaded Knitting

Beaded knitting is easier than you might think and gives a fabulously glamorous result. The key is to thread the beads onto your yarn before you begin knitting. Use either a specialized beading needle to do this or, for a budget version, take a 1 ½in (4cm) length of fuse wire, fold down the top and twist to form an eye. Use this to thread the beads directly onto your yarn.

1. First you knit across to the position of the bead. When instructions state mb (move bead), bring the yarn to the front of the work and push the bead down the yarn so that it sits next to the last stitch worked.

2. Slip the next stitch purlwise. **B**

3. Take the yarn to the back of work and knit the next stitch.

Always add the beads to a right-side row, so that they hang horizontally at the front of your work.

Knitting Effects

Swiss Darning (Duplicate Stitch)

Swiss darning is great for working small motifs because it looks as if it has been knitted into the fabric.

Horizontal Stitches: Work along the row from right to left. Bring the threaded needle to the front of the work at the base of the 'V' of the knitted stitch. Pass the needle (working from right to left) in and out of the stitch in the row above then bring the needle back to the front of the work at the base of the 'V' and push gently through to the back. Repeat for each stitch across the row.

Vertical Stitches: Work from the bottom to the top of each row. Bring the needle out at the base of the 'V' as before. Complete the stitch as for the horizontal but then bring the needle up at the base of the stitch above and continue working upwards along the line of knitted stitches.

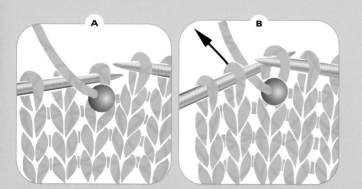

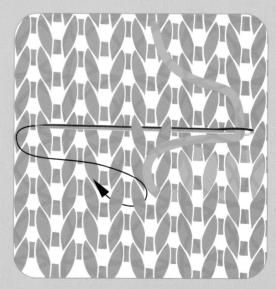

Pompoms

1. Cut out two cardboard circles a little smaller in diameter than the pompom you want. Make a hole in the middle of both, about a third of the diameter. **A**

2. Put both circles together and, using lengths of yarn, thread through the middle and begin wrapping around the outer edge until your card is completely covered. Use one or several colours for different effects. Continue in this way until the central hole is only a pinprick. **B**

3. Now for the tricky bit. With sharp-ended scissors, cut all around the edge of the circle, slicing through all the strands, then ease a longer length of yarn between the card discs and tie very firmly around the centre, leaving a tail for sewing. You have now secured all the strands of yarn around the middle. **C**

4. Gently ease the card discs over the pompom and fluff out all the strands before trimming off any loose or straggly ends. Use the long tail to sew onto the finished project.

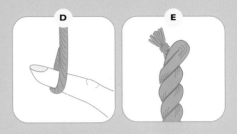

Twisted Cord

1. Cut three lengths of yarn, three times the finished length of the cord. Tie together at each end. **A**

2. Hook one end over a doorknob and, holding onto the other end, walk backwards until the strands are taut. Now, twist clockwise and keep on twisting until the cord starts to fold up on itself. **B**

3. Fold the cord in half and bring the knotted ends together; it will twist up naturally into a fat cord. Pull the knot through the original loop to secure.

Tassels

1. Cut a cardboard template a little longer than the length of tassel you want then begin wrapping your yarn – either one or several colours – a good number of times lengthways along the card.

2. When you have a bundle, thread a long strand of yarn under all the loops at the top edge of the card and tie tightly, leaving a long tail for sewing. **A**

3. Cut the wrapped strands at the opposite end of card and slide off. Wrap another length of yarn several times around the tassel head, about 1in (2.5cm) from the top. Tie tightly and trim the ends. **B**

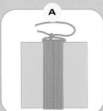

Crochet

Double Crochet

Normally, you would be making the double crochet stitch into a chain of foundation stitches. In the case of the Mod Parka (pages 62–68), though, you will need to insert the crochet hook directly into the fabric of the hood and work the double crochet stitch around the edge of the work.

Start with the right side of the hood facing you and begin at the right-hand corner edge. Insert your hook through the fabric from front to back and as close to the edge as you can and make a slip stitch as below.

Take your new yarn and wrap it round the hook from back to front. Now draw the hook back through the fabric towards you with the loop still on it. **A**

Wrap the yarn round the hook for a second time and draw the hook through the first loop on the hook. You will be left with just one loop on the hook and your first stitch. **B**

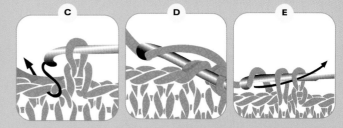

Now push the hook through your hood as before. Try to work your row of double crochet evenly through each knit stitch of the hood. Work the double crochet stitch as follows:

Wrap new yarn round the hook and draw the loop back through your work towards you. You will now have two loops on your hook. **C**

Wrap the yarn round the hook once more and draw the hook through both loops. You are now left with only one loop on your hook. This is one double crochet stitch. Continue working in this way until you reach the other end of your hood. **D**

Fasten off by breaking your yarn, threading it through your remaining loop and pulling tight. **E**

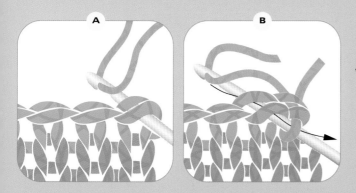

Practice makes perfect! If you are unhappy with the eveness of your crochet edging, unravel and start again.

Measuring
Your Dog

How to Measure Your Dog

You will need:

Tape measure – for measuring, of course

Pen and paper to scribble it all down – there are five measurements to remember

An extra pair of dog-friendly hands, to guide your pal into a good measuring position

A tasty snack to bribe Fido or to reward him, after the job is done

There is no such thing as an average-size dog. This fact, I found out, to my cost, during the making of this book. My first task, just as in human clothing, was to find a set of measurements to suit most average-size dogs. That way, grading the patterns would be – well, a walk in the park, right? But after measuring a huge array of canines – both large and small, pedigree and mongrel – I can tell you I was soon tearing my hair out and gnawing at my tape measure.

For instance, at what point does a small dog become a medium dog? And breeds such as bulldogs and mastiffs have large chest measurements but medium sweater-length requirements, not to mention my skinny-chested greyhound with a very long back!

It soon became obvious that, for a perfect fit, all my designs would need to have one thing in common: they would have to be adjustable. In this way, I figured each knitter could tailor the size of the sweater to their own best friend's individual needs.

For this reason, nearly every dog jacket and sweater in this book is knitted in two pieces. The idea is that you choose the pattern size that corresponds most closely to your dog's chest measurement, but then have the option to tailor the length of the garment if Fido's vital statistics don't quite match my average-sizing chart.

But before we go there, let's tackle the basics first.

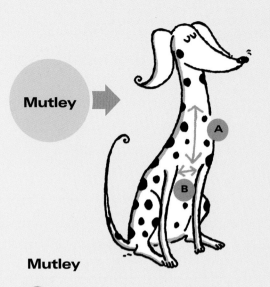

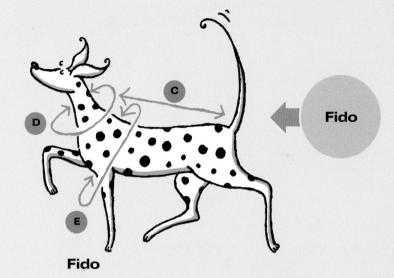

Mutley

A Distance from base of neck to top of shoulder

B Distance between two front legs

Fido

C Length from base of neck to top of tail

D Circumference around widest part of neck

E Chest circumference, around the widest part your dog's chest

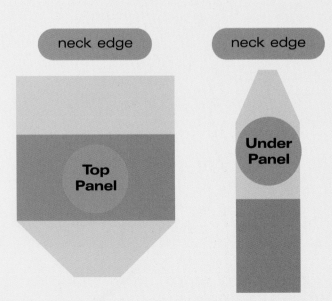

neck edge

Top Panel

neck edge

Under Panel

Length Adjustment

Lengthen/shorten here

Measurements other than those shown on the diagram at the bottom of the facing page can be easily altered, too. For instance, because the leg holes are always worked on the seams, you can move their position up or down accordingly. So, you can see the whole approach is pretty versatile.

What's Next?

Now you have your dog's unique measurements, take a look at my sizing chart below. All the sizes in the book go by these measurements. It may be that Fido's vital statistics fall neatly into one of the **XS**, **S**, **M** or **L** categories, which is fine. Go ahead and knit the pattern as it's written. But if this is not the case, start by choosing the pattern with the chest measurement that is closest to his chest size. If in doubt, select the size up. Every sweater has been designed with plenty of ease, but on the whole it is better to knit a sweater with a little extra room than one that may end up looking like a sausage casing. I talk with experience on this; I can tell you that in the instance of my own English springer

spaniel, Rusty, tight ribbing on a rather portly (okay, overweight) frame is definitely not a flattering look!

Now, begin knitting and follow the pattern until I indicate where the length adjustment should be made. You will always be shortening or lengthening the sweater beneath the leg holes at the point between the belly and the tail. Of course, you will need to take yarn requirements into consideration. If the sweater is going to be a lot longer than is standard, buy an extra ball or two just in case. Conversely, if shortening, you may not need quite as much as stated. It is all a matter of judgement.

	Chest (widest part)	**Length** (neck to tail)	**Collar** (neck girth)
XS puppies and tea-cup breeds	10in (25.5cm)	9in (23cm)	8in (20.5cm)
S pugs, daschunds, Yorkies, papillons	14in (35.5cm)	12in (30.5cm)	10in (25.5cm)
M corgis, whippets small poodles	18in (46cm)	16 (41cm)	12in (30.5cm)
L bulldog, beagle. cocker, shih tzu	22in (56cm)	21in (53.5cm)	15in (38cm)
XL lurcher, greyhound, English springer	26in (66cm)	23in (58.5cm)	17in (43.5cm)

Care Advice

Knitted Sweaters

Some of the designs in this book, such as Tiffany, Bardot and Bling, are obviously pure, over-the-top, glamour wear. If your dog is wearing one of these you probably won't be taking her for a twenty-mile romp over the moor, so it's unlikely it will need to be laundered for heavy-duty soiling. However, that said, you will want to wash them from time to time, and I recommend gently hand-washing in warm water with a non-biological detergent. Afterwards, rinse, roll up into a tea towel and gently squeeze out the excess water. Now, dry the garment flat and, when dry, give the fur a rake through with fingers or a wide-toothed comb if it's looking a little flat. Fun Fur yarns have progressed so brilliantly these days, it should look as good as new.

Many of the other designs are more practical, especially those aimed at the boys, such as Combat and Punk Vibe. These sweaters may suffer more at the paws of more boisterous dogs, but a few muddy puddles will do them little harm, and I've found the wool cycle on my washing machine brings them up as good as new. However, if in doubt, refer to the yarn label for washing instructions. Dry the garment flat as before and always check the yarn label before thinking of pressing. A general rule is to press knitted garments under a damp cloth with a low heat, but some wools are not suitable, especially those with a high acrylic content. So do be careful.

Finally, always check that buttons are attached securely before each fitting, as nobody wants their dog or puppy swallowing one whole. If you find anything loose or hanging off, then sew it back on fast and firm.

Toys and Accessories

I have used washable filling in all the toys and cushions, so you should be able to hand-wash them in non-biological detergent, just like the sweaters. When you have rinsed and squeezed out the excess water, encourage them gently back into their original shape and leave to dry.

Items such as the Kitten Mitten and the Shoe Chew have bells and other potential hazards attached, and will undoubtedly get a good mauling by your kitten or puppy. For this reason, please check your sewing is good and firm and that there are no loose pieces or leaky stuffing for your beloved pet to swallow or hurt themselves with. Remember though, they are designed to be fun, too, so common sense is the key.

Yarn Suppliers

Coats Crafts UK
(Stockists of Patons)
PO Box 22
Lingfield House,
Lingfield Point,
McMullen Road,
Darlington,
County Durham
DL1 1YQ
Tel: +44 (0)1325 394394
www.coatscrafts.co.uk

CPU Enterprises
(Stockists of Stylecraft and Sirdar)
Barncroft Villas
1 Manor House Street
Peterborough
PE1 2TL
Tel: +44 (0)1733 566617
E-mail: diane@cpu-enterprises.com
www.cpu-enterprises.com

Rowan Yarns
Green Mill Lane,
Holmfirth,
West Yorkshire.
HD 2DX
Tel: +44 (0)1484 681 881
www.rowanyarns.co.uk

Saprotex International (Pty) Ltd.
PO Box 1293
East London 5200
Fort Jackson Industrial Sites
South Africa
Tel: +27 43 7084200
www.knit1.net

Sirdar Spinning Ltd.
Flanshaw Lane,
Wakefield,
West Yorkshire.
WF2 9ND
Tel: +44 (0)1924 371501
E-mail: enquiries@sirdar.co.uk
www.sirdar.co.uk

Stylecraft
PO Box 62,
Goulbourn St.,
Keighley,
West Yorkshire
BD21 1PP
Tel: +44 (0)1535 669952

Thomas B Ramsden & Co
(Stockists of Wendy, Peter Pan, Robin)
Netherfield Rd,
Guiseley,
West Yorkshire
LS20 9PD
Tel: +44 (0)1943 872264
E-mail: sales@tbramsden.co.uk
www.tbramsden.co.uk

Abbreviations

Alt   alternate

Approx approximately

Beg   beginning

BO   bind or cast off

Cbbk   cable back

Cbfr   cable forward

Cm   centimetres

Cn   cable needle

CO   cast on

Cont   Continue

Dc   Double crochet

Dec   decrease

DK   double knit

Dpns   double pointed needles

Inc   Increase by working into front and back of same stitch

Ins   inches

K   knit

K2tog   Decrease by knitting 2 stitches together

Kwise   by knitting the st

Meas   measures

M1   Increase by picking up and knitting into the loop of the row below

MB   make a bobble

mb   move bead

P   purl

Patt   pattern

PM   place marker

P2tog   purl 2 together

PUK   pick up and knit

Rem   remaining

Rep   repeat

RH   right hand

Rnd   round

RS   right side

Sk   skip

Skpo   slip 1 st, knit 1 s, pass slipped st over (1 st decreased)

Sl   slip

Sl1p   slip one st purlwise

Sl st   slip stitch

Ssk   slip 1 knitwise, slip 1 knitwise, insert tip of left needle into front of 2 slipped sts and k2tog through back of loop.

St(s)   stitch(es)

St st   stocking stitch

Tog   together

Ws   wrong side

YO   yarn over

Yb   yarn back

Yf   yarn over

*   work instructions immediately following *, then rep. as directed.

( )   rep instructions inside brackets as many times as instructed

Conversions

Knitting Needle
Conversion Chart:

UK	Metric	US
14	**2mm**	**0**
13	2.25mm	1
12	**2.75mm**	**2**
11	3mm	-
10	**3.25mm**	**3**
-	3.5mm	4
9	**3.75mm**	**5**
8	4mm	6
7	**4.5mm**	**7**
6	5mm	8
5	**5.5mm**	**9**
4	6mm	10
3	**6.5mm**	**10.5**
2	7mm	10.5
1	**7.5mm**	**11**
O	8mm	11
00	**9mm**	**13**
OOO	10mm	15

Crochet Hook
Conversion Chart:

UK	Metric	US
8	4mm	G/6 15

Terms

UK	US
Double crochet	**Single crochet**
Cast off	Bind off
Miss	**Skip**
Tension	Gauge

Yarn Weight
UK/US Conversion Chart:

UK	US
4-ply	**Sport**
Double knitting	Light worsted
Aran	**Fisherman/ Worsted**
Chunky	Bulky
Super Chunky	**Extra Bulky8**

Acknowledgements

I would like to thank the following humans and dogs for their help in making this book.

Humans: Gill Penny-Larter at Stylecraft, **Pauline Brown** at Sirdar, **Tracy Whittington** at Patons UK, **Austen Ramsden** at Thomas B Ramsden (Wendy/ Robin/Peter Pan), **Gerrie Purcell** at GMC for seeing the potential in this book, **Dominique Page** for her editing skills, **Rebecca Mothersole** for great layout and design – the book looks fabulous, **Katherine Walker** for such wonderful illustrations of cats and dogs, **Simon Rodway** for excellent knitting and crochet illustrations, **my loving family** for support, encouragement and shameless pursuit of canine models for the cause, and finally to my wonderful husband, **Jeff**, for always being calm in the face of deadlines, encouraging in times of doubt and for having total faith in me despite not knowing a knitting needle from a crochet hook – you are my superhero and I love you.

Good luck with knitting the designs – I hope you enjoy them. And when it comes to knitting the sweaters, if in doubt about the size, make sure you read 'Measuring your Dog' and cast your mind back to those ill-fitting clothes your mother made you wear when you were tiny in the hope you would **grow into them.**

Dogs: Pip Angwin – sorry they made you bath before that snowy fitting, **Mischief Martin** – who fell asleep wearing the Punk Vibe and gave me the devil's job to remove it, **Buster Mann** – forced to try on a pink version of the Diamond Guy sweater and who will never be the same again.

My own dogs: Maisie – the perfect model looking fab in everything, **Rusty** – a plus-size model and that's putting it kindly, and, of course, in memory of **Goldie**, our rescue greyhound with terrible breath but with such a gentle, loving nature.

Goldie, without you, this book might never have been.

Index